Heleen van den Hombergh

GENDER, ENVIRONMENT AND DEVELOPMENT

a guide to the literature

Published for the Institute for Development Research Amsterdam
by International Books (Utrecht, The Netherlands), March, 1993

CIP-DATA KONINKLIJKE BIBLIOTHEEK, DEN HAAG

Hombergh, Heleen van den

Gender, environment and development : a guide to the literature / Heleen van
den Hombergh. - Utrecht : Van Arkel
Publ. in coop. with: Institute for Development Research Amsterdam. - With
index.
ISBN 90-6224-992-2
NUGI 661
Subject headings: women and environment ; bibliographies.

Cover design: Tekst/Ontwerp, Amsterdam
Cover photo: ABC, Amsterdam
Printing: Bariet, Ruinen
Production: Trees Vulto DTP en Boekproduktie, Schalkwijk

Institute for Development Research Amsterdam
Plantage Muidergracht 12, 1018 TV Amsterdam, The Netherlands
tel. 31 (0)20-5255050, fax. 31 (0)20-5255040

International Books
A. Numankade 17, 3572 KP Utrecht, The Netherlands
tel. 31 (0)30-731840, fax. 31 (0)30-733614

Contents

Preface

The Both Ends Working Group on Women and Environment, has requested InDRA (The Institute for Development Research Amsterdam) to make an inventory and set up a special collection of documentation on gender, environment and development (GED)[1].

It seemed useful to publish the results to help people interested in the subject, find their way in the large amount of literature. This report consists of introductory texts on various issues related to GED, and an extensive bibliography. I felt that an instructive guide would be more helpful than an annotated bibliography to (student) researchers, policy makers, activists, and specialists in development assistance, both from the environmental and the gender point of view. I hope this guide will inspire the readers, and stimulate an interest in theoretical issues, especially readers who work in policy-making and development assistance. To me, a tropical forester by training, some of the theory was really an eyeopener as to my own educational background. On the other hand, I hope that readers working mainly on theoretical issues will gain more insight into relevant practical areas of study, such as the influence of debt on women and the environment, or the gender perspective on local scale natural resource management.

When I told a colleague that I was working on a bibliography about gender, environment and development, she remained silent for a few seconds and then exclaimed: "...but that's everything!" I almost agree. From a wide perspective, the amount of literature on the subject is overwhelming. Yet, in this guide I try to give an overview of the literature on various issues relevant to GED. This is not another plea for recognition of the fact that women and environment are somehow connected and interdependent. This has been done, as the bibliography will show. My attempt is to systematically bring together work that may seem very diverse at first sight, but that turns out to be relevant to an understanding and operationalization of the link between gender, environment and development.

By exploring the links between different research and policy areas I hope to make a contribution to a "gender-environment-and-development-methodology" in research and policy. The guide therefore focuses more on viewpoints and policies than on facts and figures. There are limitations to my choice to provide a broad overview. It is impossible to deal with all the literature extensively.

The bibliography contains many titles that do not directly address GED. Some deal with gender and development only, others focus on environmental policy in general. If they helped me to get some grip on related themes, I chose to include them.

The bibliography serves as a first basis for InDRA's documentation on GED. Large part of of the titles in the bibliography can be found at InDRA, the rest is available in other libraries in the Netherlands (the location is added to the reference). I did not try to compile a complete bibliography. The focus is on literature available in English, whereas my collection of literature from the South is still lacking in many areas. InDRA invites you as policy makers, researchers, activists or fieldworkers to provide us with your comments, needs, and useful work you come across. Your contributions will be much appreciated.

Heleen van den Hombergh

Note

1   Definitions of the terms gender, environment and development are given in 1.1.

Acknowledgements

Writing an extensive guide to the literature within a limited amount of time requires the help of inspiring people. First of all I would like to thank Mary Boesveld for pointing out important issues in GED and for providing the documentation centre with a lot of interesting materials. Irene Dankelman has been very helpful by enabling me to screen her vast personal library. She also helped me structure the materials and define priorities for documentation and has pointed out important persons and organizations. I am grateful to documentalists Corrie Wessendorp and Joke Webbink for their help in obtaining a great deal of information. Thanks also to Sabine Haüsler and Ewa Charkiewicz-Pluta for their work concerning theoretical issues and to Douniya Loudiyi for kindly giving me a copy of her forthcoming bibliography. Loes Schenk-Sandbergen and Mirjam Letsch, Maria Muller, Suzan Blankhart and Els Klinkert, Michael Chai, Anoja Wickramasinghe, Rosemary Jommo, Noor Tabbers, Suzan Orlebeke, and Marijk Huijsman shared some of their vast knowledge and ideas with me. I am also grateful to Philomena Essed for supporting the writing process, and to Rita Gircour for her work on language and editing. Finally Jos Frijns, Marcel Hazeu, Carla Neefs, Theo van Koolwijk, Joke Schrijvers, Ange Wieberdink, and the women of the Both Ends Working Group helped greatly with their critical comments on draft versions. Some of these people will reappear in this guide because of their publications.

Information about InDRA

The aim of InDRA, the Institute for Development Research Amsterdam, is to create a multi- or interdiciplinary liaison between departments active in the field of development studies, within and beyond the University of Amsterdam. InDRA stimulates activities in development studies and development cooperation by means of joint efforts and combined resources. Through its education and research programmes, InDRA is developing and exchanging critical knowledge in order to contribute to a more just and liveable world. Senior fellow researchers from the South take part in the research projects.

InDRA's research programme contains three interdisciplinary projects:
- Youth, Poverty and Emancipation.
- Gender in a South-North Perspective.
- Environment, Development and Countervailing Power.
Gender, Environment and Development (GED) is one of the interlinking research themes. On this theme, InDRA cooperates with the Women and Development section of the Institute of Social Studies and Women's Studies of the Faculty of Arts at Utrecht University, in a project called WUMEN (Women's Umbrella network on the Environment).

At InDRA's documentation centre the special collection and documentation on Gender, Environment and Development will be further developed. If you are interested and have contributions to make you are invited to contact us. If you want to visit us to study the literature, please make an appointment by telephone at the documentation centre on Mondays, Tuesdays Wednesdays or Fridays between 10.00 and 17.00. Unfortunately it is not possible to borrow the literature.

InDRA/Institute for Development Research Amsterdam
Plantage Muidergracht 12, 1018 TV Amsterdam, The Netherlands
Tel. 31 (0)20 – 5255050, Fax. 31 (0)20 – 5255040

List of acronyms occuring in the text

CCIC	Canadian Council for International Cooperation
DAWN	Development Alternatives with Women for a New Era, a network of Southern women researchers (Barbados)
DGIS	Directoraat Generaal Internationale Samenwerking (General Directorate for International Cooperation), part of Dutch Ministry of Foreign Affairs
ELC(I)	Environment Liaison Centre (International), Global Coalition for Environment and Development (Nairobi)
ESMAP	Energy Sector Management Assistance Program
FAO	Food and Agricultural Organization of the United Nations (Rome)
FSR/E	Farming Systems Research and Extension (methodology)
GAD	Gender and Development
GATT	General Agreement on Tariffs and Trade
GED	Gender, Environment and Development
HIVOS	Humanistisch Instituut voor Ontwikkelings Samenwerking (Humanist Institute for Development Cooperation), Dutch funding organization (the Hague)
ILO	International Labour Organization/also International Labour Office (Geneva)
InDRA	Institute for Development Research Amsterdam (Amsterdam)
INSTRAW	UN International Institute for Research and Training for the Advancement of Women (Santo Domingo)
IRC	International Research Centre for Water and Sanitation, (the Hague)
ISS	Institute for Social Studies (the Hague)
IUCN	International Union for the Conservation of Nature and Natural Resources (Gland)
NGO	Non Governmental Organization
OECD/DAC	Development Assistance Committee of the Organization for Economic Cooperation and Development. Including Expert Group on Women in Development (Paris)

9

PrepCom	Meetings of Preparatory Committee for UNCED (number I to IV)
SWAGSD	Senior Women's Advisory Group on Sustainable Development; advisors to UNEP
UNCED	United Nations Conference on Environment and Development, held in June '92 (Rio de Janeiro).
UNCTAD	United Nations Conference on Trade and Development
UNDP	United Nations Development Programme (New York)
UNEP	United Nations Environmental Programme (Nairobi)
UNIFEM	United Nations Development Fund for Women (New York)
USAID	United States Agency for International Development (Washington)
VENA	Onderzoeks en Documentatiecentrum Vrouwen en Autonomie (Research and Documentation Centre Women and Autonomy) (Leiden)
VROM	Ministerie voor Volkshuisvesting Ruimtelijke Ordening en Milieu (Dutch Ministery of Housing, Physical Planning and Environment)
WCED	World Commission on Environment and Development (Brundtland Commission)
WED	Women, Environment and Development
WEDNET	Women, Environment and Development Network, network of researchers from Africa and Canada, coordinated by ELCI (Nairobi)
WEDO	Women's Environment and Development Organization (New York)
WEN	Women's Environmental Network (London)
WHO	World Health Organization (Geneva)
WID	Women In Development (USAID)
WWF	World Wildlife Fund (Geneva)

List of important events

1962   Rachel Carson's book "Silent Spring"
1970   Ester Boserup's book "Women's role in economic development"
1972   Meadows et al. release "The limits to growth"
1972   UN Conference on the Human Environment (Stockholm)
1975   International Women's Year; start of the UN Decade for Women
1980   World Conservation Strategy (IUCN/WWF/UNEP)
1985   UN conference to Review and Appraise the Decade for Women
        (Nairobi)
        NGO parallel conference: Forum '85
1987   "Our Common Future" (Brundtland report, WCED)
1987   Conference on Women and the World Conservation Strategy
        (IUCN, Gland)
1990   Regional Follow Up conferences "Action to Our Common
        Future"
        NGO parallel Women's Forum in Bergen
1991   "Caring for the Earth", Second World Conservation Strategy
        IUCN/WWF/UNEP)
        Preparatory Committee meetings for United Nations
        Conference on Environment and Development
1991   NGO conference to prepare for UNCED "Roots of the Future"
        (Paris)
1991   UNEP's Global Assembly on Women and the Environment
        "Partners in Life" (Miami)
        NGO conference "World Women's Congress for a Healthy
        Planet" (Miami)
1992   United Nations Conference on Environment and Development
        (UNCED)
        NGO parallel conference "Global Forum"

PART I

Introduction and literature review
on gender, environment and development

CHAPTER I

Introduction

Since the late '80s the connection between Gender, Environment and Development (GED) has been emerging as an area of special interest for researchers, policy makers and activists. GED as a theme has been extended from occasional research and scattered activism into a worldwide NGO network, and entered the rhetoric at the highest levels of international policy. But what does it really mean to deal with the three elements in combination, and do justice to them all? In the first paragraph the subject is introduced by taking a stand on that. In the second paragraph the structure of this guide is outlined. For an introduction to the field, a brief historical overview of how GED has become recognized as a special area of concern is clarifying. For this purpose, some major landmarks on GED in international policy are discussed in the third paragraph.

1.1 Taking a stand on the issue of GED

What are the implications of linking gender, environment and development? What issues and problems are relevant when trying to establish such links? In order to answer these questions it is crucial to explain some of the terminology used.

Gender
The term gender as it is used here, refers to culturally and historically specific concepts of femininity and masculinity, and the power relations between men and women *(Schrijvers* 1993). Gender is not the same as sex, it refers to the social construction of sex roles and relations between the sexes[1]. Gender may imply that men must be the head of the family, that women are not allowed to cut trees, that women are the ones primarily responsible for children's health and education, that men and women have their own different tasks and spheres of decision-making, etcetera. Along with factors such as class, age, race, and ethnicity, gender

is a fundamental concept in understanding human behaviour and social processes.

Because gender is also fundamental in understanding human interaction with the environment, it is better to focus on gender than to focus on women only. With respect to natural resources gender shapes the sexual division of labour, knowledge, responsibility and control. Because of gender, women play a special role in managing these resources. Therefore, a large amount of the literature deals with women specifically. WED (Women, Environment and Development) has become a key concept. In this guide much special attention will be paid to women's roles, and women's problems. But it is done from a gender point of view. Except from being culturally and historically specific, gender is shaped by ideological, religious, ethnic and economic determinants, and shows differences between classes and societies. (e.g. *Moser* 1989-1, *French* 1985 or *Haraway* 1991). However, some general features in the relation between gender and environment can be found.

Environment
The term environment in this guide refers primarily to natural resources, but I emphasize their close relation with the macroeconomic, political and cultural environment. The term environment has been criticized, and so has the term natural resources, because they are both perceived as reflecting an antropocentric view: the environment of man, natural resources meant for humans. (e.g. *King* 1989, *Wiertsema* 1991). Therefore, some choose to speak of "ecology" instead. This term refers to the knowledge about the relationships between organisms and their physical environment. In fact, ecology is a field of study, but it is often used to describe the perception of the interdependence of living creatures (human and non-human) and their natural environment. Thus, the term ecology has also obtained a normative connotation, and with this in mind one can look to environment at large from an ecological point of view. Then it is relevant to stress the interdependence of nature, culture, economics and politics.

Development
Development, in general, refers to economic, socio-political and cultural processes of change in human societies *(Schrijvers* 1993). The term development in GED has different meanings and connotations. It may refer to development as it has taken place, caused by efforts towards

economic development, the intended transition from poverty to wealth, a process mainly steered by Northern countries. This understanding of development has a negative connotation for GED, because it often has meant "maldevelopment" (a term used by *Shiva* 1989): impoverishment of the majority in Southern countries, women in particular, and unsustainable exploitation of the natural resource base.

The term development also can have a positive connotation. Development can be seen as an ideal: in which case it is often referred to as sustainable development (see 1.2, 3.2 etc.) which should reverse the negative trends mentioned above. The term development may also refer to efforts of development cooperation in "developing countries", efforts that may either contribute to sustainable development or maldevelopment. It is useful to keep the scope wide enough to elaborate on all three connotations in this guide.

The term development occurs in the text mainly in the first connotation (economic development) unless otherwise specified. GED will be dealt with as a global issue, but the special focus is on gender and environment in Southern countries. The following is meant to explain why.

GED links
The literature shows that three strongly interrelated factors are important to explain why gender, environment and development are so closely connected. These are the sexual division of labour, the "feminization of poverty" and gender ideology.

The *sexual division of labour* makes women, especially poor rural women in the South, important contributors to agriculture, and often makes them solely responsible for the collection of firewood, fodder and water. This sexual division of labour implies that women and men have different domains of knowledge on the use and management of natural resources, and different interests in these matters. Women's knowledge about the environment is often more comprehensive, because of the diversity of their tasks. The main responsibility for sustaining the family is usually assigned to the women, increasingly so because of male migration away from degraded rural areas. This makes women's knowledge an important issue in environmental management and rehabilitation.

Poor people in the South are the first to suffer from environmental problems because they are so directly dependent on natural resources, often non-privately owned resources, for their livelihood. The

17

"feminization of poverty" implies that the worldwide crisis of environment and development, combined with the male bias in development policies and cooperation, have caused the relatively stronger impoverishment among women. This is not to say that women have not been poor before, but their situation has actually even worsened.

Because of the sexual division of labour, and the feminization of poverty, it is often the women who bear the heaviest burden of environmental degradation. The decline in soil fertility and in food, fodder and firewood supplies make women's workloads grow heavier and heavier. First this affects their own health, and shortly after, the health of their families. Eventually, women's inability to sustain livelihood is detrimental to the health of a society as a whole.

An important factor in all this is the prevailing *gender ideology*, which defines women's subordinate position. At the local level this mostly implies that women have less access to and control over resources than men. Poor women, no matter how inventive and knowledgeable, are, more often than men, deprived of the possibility to use and manage natural resources in a sustainable way. This inequality in access and control thus frustrates the capacity of poor women to sustain livelihood, and at the same time hampers their contribution to sustainable environmental management. Their responsibilities, and the obstacles put in their way make that women tend to be the first to protest and take action against developments causing environmental degradation.

Women, however, often lack the decision-making power over the use of resources and the direction of development in general. Not only at the local level, but in all spheres and at all levels of decision-making. Therefore a global perspective on GED is needed, to which I will come back later.

Labels in the literature
The literature mainly deals with poor rural women in the South, who get all kinds of labels referring to their relation to the environment. In most publications they are identified as the first victims of environmental degradation. Sometimes they are called contributors to degradation (e.g. *Clones/World Bank* 1991), often with the remark that they have no other choice. However, their contribution to degradation mostly results from their problematic position *(Dankelman and Davidson* 1988 etc). Also, it should be emphasized that the damage to the environment caused by poor peasant women is not comparable to the

damage caused by the side effects of the green revolution, failing land reforms, and the destruction of ecosystems for export, to benefit the prosperity in the North *(Wieberdink/InDRA* 1991).

Poor rural women have also been identified as "day-to-day environmental managers" *(Dankelman and Davidson* 1988), or "barefoot conservationalists", *(Davidson* 1989) They have been recognized as possible beneficiaries of environmental projects *(Davidson* 1990). *Rocheleau* (1990) discusses the ideas of women as "victims, villains and fixers" of the environment. *Rodda* (1991) calls women "protesters against environmental destruction, and potential agents of change towards sustainable development, being producers, consumers, campaigners, educators and communicators". No lack of labels for their roles.

Abzug (in *Linggard and Moberg* 1990) calls women "the most neglected and valuable natural resource". This idea can easily be interpreted as "they should be utilized more". In many publications women are implicitly called instruments for environmental protection. Sometimes this is clearly done strategically to convince policy makers. *Dankelman and Davidson* (1988), for instance, talk about "investing in women as a major resource for improving the environment". Often, however, this instrumental way of dealing with women reflects a gender-blind and short-sighted view on environmental rehabilitation. The conclusion from the above is that if one chooses to speak in terms of resource use, poor women in the South are "overexploited", as is shown by the evidence about their burden and resulting health problems (e.g. *Sims/WHO* 1990, *Dankelman* 1991-1, see 5.1). As *Gita Sen and Caren Grown* (1985/87) point out clearly: "It should be remembered that women are neither responsible for the crisis in the world system, nor can they be expected to resolve it".

GED and power, a global perspective
Gender shapes the sexual division of labour, the differences between men's and women's knowledge, responsibility and control in the area of natural resources, and -thus- it shapes all those labels for women. Some glorify their potential, others are downright humiliating. The gendered division may have been a crucial survival strategy of many societies, and thus an important factor to study in efforts to contribute to sustainable development. At the same time, it often reflects the subordinate position of women, a situation which is aggravated by gender-blind external influences. Gender in relation to natural resources and to the economic, political and cultural environment is probably most evident as a

19

dimension of power, besides class, age, ethnicity and religion. Changing the existing power dimensions is crucial for attaining sustainable development. For ethical and humanitarian reasons, but also because both luxury (waste of resources) and poverty (overexploitation of the leftovers) contribute largely to environmental degradation.

This brings us to a statement found in many theoretical writings. Gender as a dimension of power may also have played a role in the creation of the Western development model which has been so detrimental to both women and the natural environment, especially in the South. Environmental degradation on the one hand, and the feminization of poverty on the other are caused by or reinforced by male-biased development, based on a model of exploitation of resources mainly for the prosperity of Northern countries and Southern elites. The image of the world as an object to be mastered by men prevails in discussions about the future of the earth (for example in the United Nations Conference on Environment and Development; *UNCED* 1992). This world view has sanctioned the simultaneous marginalization of nature and women, who have always been closely associated (see 3.3). Recognizing the historical roots of this fundamental conceptional flaw – to put it euphemistically – is crucial in working towards sustainable development. Therefore, the gender factor must not only be taken into account in examining or planning the use of natural resources on a local scale, but also in examining the dominant ideology on how to deal with the environment and development on a global scale. This, however, makes some radicals put the world into a biologically deterministic one-liner: men destroy nature and women defend it. We must also keep in mind that other factors such as class and nationality may play a more crucial role than gender. And that there is a tension between general insights in GED, and the specific, ever changing relations, interests and needs of people as social actors in specific cultural and historical circumstances.

To some extent, the factors mentioned above: sexual division of labour, feminization of poverty and gender ideology are also important for the relationship of Northern women to the environment. In the industrialized countries, as well as in the South, women are responsible for caring and feeding, they are overrepresented in the low income categories, and underrepresented in decision-making bodies. Women may also have specific health risks, and may be harder hit by government initiated financial measures and cuts in services for the sake of the environment. Although certain of these features concern poor people in general, they may cause solidarity between women especially. However, some interests of women in the North are opposed to interests of women in the South. For example, Dutch women may want cheap coffee and poor African women want good prices for products from sustainable agriculture. Since Northern women are responsible for much of domestic household consumption they have a lot of influence on production patterns, both in their own and in Southern countries. Their consumer power may be an effective instrument for change, although it should be emphasized that changing production and consumption patterns is not women's responsibility alone. Despite the differences, there is growing international solidarity between women active in environmental issues, as the NGO process towards UNCED has shown (see 1.3, 2.2 etc.).

In the development of GED policies in North, South and East, women should not be used as a "human resource" for environmental rehabilitation. It is important to find concepts and strategies of development, that will benefit both the position of women and the environment. This will not occur spontaneously. If the labour and knowledge of Southern women are used in reforestation to control erosion, and the women end up without say over the land and the trees afterwards, they benefit only marginally from it. A similar discrepancy between environmental rehabilitation and women's scope of action can be observed in a Northern context. For example a cutback in the mobility of cars (e.g. by higher prices or regulations) could cut back the participation of Dutch women in the labour force, and consequently in decision-making. Because women often have the primary responsibility for the household and the children next to their paid jobs, a car may be perceived as indispensable. Such perceived "discrepancies" between environmental and women's interests stem from the gender role ascribed to women. Also these conflicts of interests are surmountable. In the first example, handing over the control of the newly planted areas to women would probably benefit both their position and the management of the resource. In the second example, better public transport facilities would benefit both women's participation in the labour force and the fight against pollution. And, men, of course, could also contribute more to the household and education of the children. Therefore it is crucial to integrate environmental and emancipatory policy; eventually the benefits will reinforce each other.

What does this all mean for this guide? First, that improving women's position and the state of the environment are considered equally important. The literature discussed contributes to an understanding how gender inequalities and environmental care are intertwined in history, crisis situations and possible "ways out". Descriptions of how economic and/or "mal"-development have influenced gender and the environment are presented, as well as ideas on how sustainable development, beneficial to both the position of women and the natural environment can be achieved. My focusing on gender does not mean that I only discuss literature that focuses on gender instead of women; that would mean skipping half of the bibliography. Finally, I stress that the issue of GED should be dealt with on much more than just the household or local level. These views are meant to be reflected in my choice of subjects, references, and in the comments.

1.2 Structure and use of the guide

Next chapter is written to provide the reader with some of the possible introductions to the subject (chapter 2). Recommendations for more specialized introductory reading will be made in the other chapters. The structure of the remainder of this guide is in fact based on key questions that follow from the GED links sketched above. Which theories have been influential in the GED debates? Which ideologies have prevailed in the development model that has been so detrimental to both women and the environment, and which ideas support a transformation? In chapter 3 critiques of science and development, and various approaches in philosophy and development cooperation will be discussed briefly to introduce the reader to this extensive field of study.

Chapter 4 deals with the global issues that are still reflecting the continuous marginalization of women and environment, problems which need to be addressed for a structural change to sustainable development. Factors on the national level will be discussed in this chapter, but will not be dealt with seperately.

It is essential to elaborate on the relationship between gender and environment at the local level, to identify the possibilities and constraints that face women in the use and management of natural resources, factors which research and policy should catch on to. For this purpose two representative issues are discussed in chapter 5; health and natural resource management.

Next, what policy steps are being taken with respect to women, gender and environment? (chapter 6). How then to transform analysis, policy and projects conform a gender-and-environment-methodology? Chapter 7 focuses on some conceptual and analytical tools. Which movements are attempting to combat environmental degradation and gender inequality in combination (chapter 8)?

The literature offers no clear answers to all these questions, but it provides ideas about the direction in which they could be found. In the last chapter some blind spots in literature are identified and some recommendations are made to academics and policy makers (chapter 9).

The bibliography contains more references than are discussed in the text. Readers interested in literature on specific subjects, can use the alphabetical subject index at the end in addition.

The focus is on literature in English, but some Dutch and other contributions are also included. Throughout the guide, attention will be paid to "our own" Dutch policy on gender, environment and development, especially in international cooperation, which may be of special interest for Dutch readers, and others working in or with the Netherlands. The next paragraph, however, focuses on the attention for GED in international policy.

1.3 International policy: some landmarks

In the process towards recognition of the GED link, critical researchers, development workers and grassroots movements have played a catalytic role. In this paragraph the focus is on how this recognition process is reflected in international policy writings. We need to go back some 20 years for the "discovery" of environment and women in political circles. As one can see, "women and development" and "environment and development" have been seperate tracks for a long time.

Attention for women
Most historical overviews on women and development mention *Ester Boserup* as the motor in the recognition of women's role in economic development (1970, reprint 1989). She was the first to highlight the

productive roles of poor rural women in the South, and show how women had been negatively affected by development while men had benefited from it. She inspired many researchers to investigate the gender dimension of development. Moreover, her work was a catalyst for announcing the International Women's Year in 1975 and the following "UN Decade for Women" (1975-1985), in which special efforts were made to "integrate" women in development. However, the Decade failed to directly benefit women, mainly because of major misconceptions about gender and development (for example, that development efforts focusing on men would equally benefit women and children), and because of the devastating effects of several global factors like the debt problem (see 4.2).[2] The achievement of the Decade may be the recognition of the essential role of women in development, both as beneficiairies and contributers *(Dankelman and Davidson* 1988). The UN Conference to Review and Appraise the Decade for Women outlined measures to fulfill the demand for equality and integration of women into mainstream economic development, in a document called the "Forward Looking Strategies For the Advancement of Women" (or "Forward Looking Strategies", *UN* 1986).

Ever since, the attention for women's problems and environmental concerns alike has been chanelled through special purpose-built institutions, mainly focusing on project level, often lacking any real political influence. Since the late '80s gender has become a key area of concern. *Caroline Moser* (1989-1) and *Noeleen Heyzer* (1991) have provided an overview of different approaches to Women in Development as they evolved over the years (see also 3.1)

Attention for the environment
Environmentalism as a movement in the North began in the 19th century as a response to the effects of industrialization. At first it was essentially synonymus with wildlife conservation. In the 1960s the environment became a topic in the protest movement against the military industrial complex. *Rachel Carson's* book "Silent Spring" (1962, reprint 1977) about the devastating effects of broad spectrum pesticides is often mentioned as a landmark in environmental consciousness.

The establishment also felt it had to reflect on the other side of the coin of modernization. This led to the first major international conference on the environment, the UN conference on the Human Environment in Stockholm in 1972, where the United Nations Environmental Programme (UNEP) was initiated *(Arts and Berghuizen*

1992). The focus was global, but the conference was merely meant to deal with the Northern environmentalist issues evident by that time, such as pollution. A preparatory meeting of experts was held in Founex, Switzerland, to bridge some of the (conceptual) gaps between environment and development concerns, and to get Southern countries interested in the conference. At the Founex meeting, and later at the Stockholm Conference itself, the link between poverty and environmental degradation was made, caught in the phrase "the pollution of poverty". But this was not discussed in great detail, and no clear action was outlined. The conference stated the need to resolve "conflicts between environment and development" without demonstrating how *(Adams* 1990).

At the same time, the publication of "The limits to growth" *(Meadows et al.* 1972) had a considerable impact on the thinking about environment and development by emphasizing the finiteness of natural resources and thus the constraints to the current lifestyle and naming population growth as one of the major threats to the world's survival. This became a dominating concept in influential international policy events and documents later on (especially since the Brundtlandt report, see below).

The World Conservation Strategy, launched in 1980 *(IUCN/UNEP/WWF* 1980) inspired many countries to develop national conservation strategies, the Netherlands among them. According to the Strategy, conservation contributes to development, and development to conservation. But the strategy applied mainly to the local, and not the global scale of development.

In 1987 the World Commission on Environment and Development, the "Brundtland Commission" published its well-known report "Our Common Future" (WCED 1987). This report had a much greater impact than the World Conservation Strategy. WCED gave a strong impulse to the environmental concerns in development by reviving the concept of sustainable development with the celebrated definition: "Development that meets the needs of the present generations without compromising the ability of future generations to meet their needs". WCED places this concept within the economic and political context of international development. The report has inspired many, but it also received a lot of criticism especially because of the belief in economic growth as a precondition for sustainability *(Adams* 1990[3]).

In 1990 regional follow up conferences were held, under the umbrella "Action to our Common Future" (see *Starke* 1990). In 1991 a new World

Conservation Strategy appeared, in which the scope was widened from conservation to sustainable development *(IUCN/UNEP/WWF* 1991).

Twenty years after Stockholm, the United Nations Conference on Environment and Development *(UNCED)* took place in Rio de Janeiro in 1992. Whereas Stockholm drew attention to the fact that international efforts were needed to prevent environmental collapse, this conference was meant to bring about action and regulations, mainly based on the analysis of the Brundtland report. The outcomes were a non-legally binding statement about forests worldwide, and two binding conventions on climate change and biological diversity (the Bush administration, however, failed to sign the latter because of its perceived national interests). Furthermore, there is the "Declaration of Rio", which is merely a framework of ideas, and "Agenda 21" an extensive document listing points of action towards the next century *(UNCED* 1992-1/2). So guidelines have been formulated; but the process of achieving binding agreements has been very problematic. Big obstacles in Rio were the problem of finances – it has been suggested that the costs to organize the meeting exceed the total of the financial commitments made – and the conflicting ideological and economic interests of North vs South, European Community vs Bush Administration and others.

However, this event has mobilized many NGOs around the world. Despite the differences the NGOs formulated various alternatives for sustainable development and concluded alternative treaties on the subjects dealt with in UNCED (see e.g. *ELCI* 1992-1/2, and *Pollard et al.* 1992). There has also been an interesting lobby to get women on the UNCED agenda, and interesting women's forums in the preparatory process, which will be dealt with later. Before doing so I will sketch the recent coming together of women's and environmental concerns in international policy.

Attention for women and environment
Social movements in the South have played a major role in bringing about the recognition that the three elements in GED are interconnected. The first international meeting on the subject "Women, environment and development" was an NGO workshop in Nairobi 1985 (see: *ELC/Forum* '85, 1986), parallel to the UN Conference to Review and Appraise the Decade for Women. This workshop, an initiative of UNEP,

revealed why and how women in developing countries were hit by the international environmental crisis.

In the "Forward Looking Strategies" of the official UN conference, the environment was mentioned as an area of concern for women (UN 1986). One of the resolutions urges "Women to be more conscious of the crucial role they play in environmental and natural resource management", and requests the UNEP to provide information on how women can play an active role in combatting serious environmental problems.

For that purpose UNEP installed a Senior Women's Advisory Group on Sustainable Development (SWAGSD) shortly afterwards. In the years that followed this group organized four Regional Assemblies to engage women in the assesment of the environmental condition in their respective regions, advance their networking, and review regional blueprints for environmental action divised by the ministries in the regions. The Global Assembly, in 1991, was held to demonstrate women's capacities in environmental management, and to contribute to the advancement of "affordable, sustainable, visible and repeatable" environmental management. 218 project "success stories" (reviewed in advance) were published. These were analyzed to come to five regional action plans for the repetition of projects, and come up with recommendations to governments, the academic world etc, to support these plans (see: *Global Assembly* 1991 and 1992).

Right after the Global Assembly, the "World Women's Congress for a Healthy Planet" took place (see: *World Women's Congress* 1991-1/1992). This congress was in fact the NGO answer to the Global Assembly, and primarily intended to give voice to a women's perspective on UNCED. Where the Assembly was interesting for its case studies, this congress was interesting for showing the growing awareness of the effects of global processes and structures on the issue of women and environment. The core of this event were "tribunals" in which various witnesses on women and the environment were heard. An alternative to UNCED's "Agenda 21" was produced, the "Women's Action Agenda 21". This Agenda propagates change on many interrelated issues. Also regional meetings were held, which showed the various priorities and action plans on environment and development of women from different backgrounds. The congress showed that the environment cannot be saved without thorough transformation, for which three guiding principles can be identified: global equity, resource ethics and the empowerment of women *(World Women's Congress* 1992, see also 2.2).

There has been a strong lobby to convince UNCED officials to recognize the role of women in environment and development. In the Third preparatory meeting, a resolution on Women, Environment and Development *(UNCED/Prepcom III* 1991-1) was easily agreed upon internationally. A real success for the lobby or a sign that it is still a very marginal terrain posing no threats, only benefits? In Prepcom III, women are called "active and equal participants in the process of ecosystem management and control of environmental degradation". As a special cross-cutting issue the resolution was integrated into the final documents for "Agenda 21" and The Declaration of Rio de Janeiro *(UNCED* 1992-1/2 worked out in 6.1).

It remains to be seen what the UNCED's recognition of women's crucial role in environment and development will imply for international and national policies. This cannot be seen apart, of course, from the overall implementation of the ideas formulated at UNCED, which will not be without problems.

It is to be expected however, that the agreements made by environmental and women's movements from all over the world, agreements which are reflected in the results of the *World Women's Congress* (1991/1992), the NGO preparatory meeting for UNCED "Roots of the Future" ("Agenda Ya Wananchi", *ELCI* 1992), and the NGO shadow conference during UNCED "Global Forum" (see *Pollard et al.* 1992) will have an impact. Perhaps not so much on international policy directly, but as a growing worldwide movement expressing and uniting the views "from below".

Notes

1 *Joyce Outshoorn* (1989) argues that because in ideology, gender (social) and sex (biological) are two different concepts, the concept of gender in feminism runs the risk of reproducing the dichotomy between nature and culture (see paragraph on ecofeminism). However, sex and gender are closely connected.
2 Studies have shown that the socio-economic status of women has worsened considerably during the decade *(Sen and Grown* 1987, see further 4.1 and 4.2).
3 *Adams* (1990) gives a very extensive overview over the history of environment and (sustainable) development thinking

CHAPTER 2

Overview of introductory literature

Some publications may serve as useful introductions for anyone interested in the subject. This chapter makes some suggestions for first reading. The first paragraph deals with three valuable books on women, environment and development. Each book introduces the subject from a different angle. The second paragraph deals with some conference papers and proceedings (especially by NGOs). They are useful for additional reading because they are a rich source of case-studies and personal stories. They also reveal the ideas behind the lobby of international politics on the subject, and its achievements. In the last paragraph some specialized readers and issues of magazins are mentioned, which contain interesting articles or interviews on GED.

2.1 Introductory books

Irene Dankelman and Joan Davidson (1988) have written a very useful book: "Women and environment in the Third World; alliance for the future". In the first part the authors elaborate on the crucial role women play in the management of natural resources because of their traditional tasks in food production, the provision of water, energy, and fodder. They show that because of their tasks, and of their being the poorest of the poor, women are the hardest hit by environmental degradation (also in the urban environment). The second part discusses how women have organized for change and how the international world responded. The book is a plea for development institutions to recognize women's crucial role, their difficulties and their initiatives, illustrated by numerous case-studies and interviews. The idea is that women's ecological knowledge, ability to cooperate and educational tasks in the so-called Third World are central to sustainable development, and that their position should be strengthened. The book may serve as a practical "handbook". It is practical for users ("what do the authors say about energy?") and practical in the sense that it provides a lot of facts and figures, but it does not provide for an explicit analysis of the roots of the development failures which underly the reality that is presented. In their criticism of the book, *Arts & van Reisen* (1988) try to make the major underlying ideas explicit. They accuse the authors of connecting environmental and women's interests too easily, of lacking a political-economic view, and of overvaluing the small and traditional.[1] Indeed, that is why one should not stick to this handbook only, and read some theory and elaborations on the wider context of GED.

Annabel Rodda in her book "Women and the environment" (1991) focuses more on the environment than Dankelman and Davidson (who focus more on women), describing and interconnecting environmental problems and their consequences for the fulfillment of "human and basic" needs, from macro- to microlevel. The book contains a list of organizations and a guide to education and action. Rodda has included a special chapter in which she explains some key concepts and problems concerning the environment, using many diagrammes and charts. It is a good overview for the layperson, but in describing the causes and solutions of issues such as deforestation, population pressure and (causes of) disasters she does not go much beyond top-down technical solutions. This is because she quotes many experts who deny the causal role of the North in environmental degradation, and who fail to recognize the possible role of grassroot initiatives in sustainable development. Rodda connects the role of the North only with more evident issues such as militarization, biotechnology and debt. Further on in her book her views on environmental issues and the crucial role of women proves to be less mainstream, but especially because of the chapter on large scale environmental problems, she does not fully succeed in the difficult task of making the connections between large and smaller scale processes clear. A challenge for the next writer of a book on GED?

Vandana Shiva's controversial book "Staying alive; women, ecology and development" (1989) introduces the subject by looking at the roots of what she calls "maldevelopment". With the women of India as an example, she tries to lay bare the roots of this maldevelopment that has been oppressive to both women and nature: Western patriarchy and its reductionist science. Western science establishes a monopoly on knowledge for economic pursuit only, and is totally inadequate to deal with nature.[2]

Shiva's "feminine principle" meaning harmony, sustainability and diversity, as practiced by local Indian women, should become the counterforce of this maldevelopment. "The recovery of the feminin principle is an intellectual and political challenge to maldevelopment as a patriarchal project of domination and destruction, of violence and subjugation, of dispossession and the dispensability of both women and nature". Shiva is one of the most prominent spokespersons of "ecofeminism"[3].

Some critics have given useful nuances to her statement. She has been criticized e.g. for obscuring much earlier roots of patriarchy in antiquity and Indian culture *(Dietrich* 1988-2, on Shiva's earlier but similar work), and for leaving such topics as the subjugation of tribal peoples by mainstream Indian culture, or the conflicting interests of men and women in the village society undiscussed *(Nathan* 1990 on forestry). *Bina Agarwal* (1988-2), does not directly criticize Shiva, but analyzes the impact of patriarchy in India, which Shiva's work is lacking.

Shiva is also criticized for assuming that women are the only "knowers" or activists on environmental matters *(van den Hoven* 1990), and for idealizing women as natural saviours of the environment *(Haüsler and Charkiewicz-Pluta* 1991-1). However, Shiva's emphasis on the special reciprocal bond between women and nature does not mean that she argues that women have the sole possibility and responsibility for environmentally sound development. The principle is more an answer to western reductionist science and development. An extensive summary and critique is written by *Harsh Sethi* (1989). Sethi argues that what is disturbing in Shiva's argument is "the tendency to dramatize, to present as facts what are still contested views, and a certain restructuring of history into preordained concepts". Shiva does indeed tend to romanticize traditional society, and to shut out anything large scale or foreign, which may be unrealistic and unattainable. Still, the book may be a real eyeopener and serve as a mirror for all those who work in science and international cooperation.

2.2 Conference papers and proceedings

I recommend studying the proceedings of important events, (chapter 1, see also overview page 11). The report of the first international meeting on GED, an NGO workshop in Nairobi in 1985 *(ELC/Forum '85 1986)* is a collection of interesting statements and case-studies from all over the world, featuring such "leading ladies" of the environmental movement as Wangari Maathai (Green Belt Movement Kenia, see chapter 8), and

Vandana Shiva. However, even more impressive are the personal talks for example of Sithembo Nyoni, who links the declined food security in Africa with national and international mismanagement, and with dependency on external inputs.

The ELC report contains many more and less matured seeds of the discussions that can be found in more recent writings, such as the effects of global development on the local level and the possibilities for incorporating the local perspective into higher levels of decision-making. Helena Landazuri, speaking about Latin America, emphasizes the active role of women as conservationists, educators, and researchers. Mary Ann Eriksen wrote in her introduction: "women have been the great leaders and organizers of grassroots action, but we have not often wielded much power beyond that level".

In the final statement of the workshop it is argued that the ecological crisis is emerging from a non-sustainable model, which is capital intensive, pyramidical in its decision-making process and large project oriented. This model favours participation of men as single representatives of the family unit. It concludes that the growth of women's power and the sustainability of development are "ecologically tied". The report is an impressive document including relevant parts of the official UN Conference, and its "Forward Looking Strategies" (UN 1986).

Another report, which presents many ideas and is suitable for integral reading is from the Women's Forum (Linggard and Moberg 1990). This meeting was organized parallel to a regional UN Follow up Conference of the World Commission on Environment and Development "Action to our Common Future", where women were severely underrepresented. The report of the Women's Forum contains summaries of speeches in which the need for structural changes are far more eloquently argued than in the ELC report. Berit As critically reviews the Brundtland report (WCED 1987) from a women's studies perspective. She states that besides the lack of connection between its fundamental attitudes and its recommendations, the Brundtland report lacks an analysis of the factors causing the development which the report is warning for: patriarchy and capitalism. Margrit Kennedy proposes a new monetary system aimed at qualitative growth. Fakhra Salimi argues the need of a new system of values, stating that, for instance, racism is as much a pollutant as industrial waste.

UNEP's *Global Assembly* on Women and the Environment (1991) has produced a vast amount of "success stories": case-studies on women's actions for the environment. 218 "success stories" are published on women and energy, waste, water management and environmentally friendly systems, products and technologies. The main document contains a huge list of addresses from grassroots women involved in the "success stories".

The discrepancy between the technocratic, top-down speeches held at this Assembly by international policy makers and (most of) the actions by women at the grassroots level, which were selected beforehand, may be illustrative of the gap that exists between these two different levels of activity.[4] A real must for policy makers seeking to bridge this gap, is the Special Report compiled after the *Global Assembly* (1992-1), with the findings, recommendations and action plans. It contains numerous recommendations, e.g. for strengthening women's environmental management at the local level, and for stimulating women's participation in environmental policy making. Also interesting are the reports of the Regional Assemblies, held in preparation of the Global Assembly. See *Loudiyi et al.* (1988) for the African Assembly, and *Ofosu-Amaah* (1991) for the Latin American and Carribean Assembly.

The report of a regional South Asian workshop to prepare for UNCED and to counteract the Northern dominated agenda *(Bhasin et al.* 1991) reflects the search for a regional response to the environment and development crisis. A feminist perspective is implicit in the discussions, which take local initiatives as their starting point.

Even more of a must for policy makers and activists is the final report of the *World Women's Congress for a Healthy Planet* (1991/1992). Michele Landsberg gives a vivid overview of the congress with many examples of statements and facts that were put forward. She provides summaries of the testimonies of the 15 women "witnesses" on environmental matters who were heard in the tribunal. The testimonies themselves however are more convincing when read integrally (or heard on tape!) They deal with such matters as radioactive military waste, logging, debt, biotechnology, alternative economics, human rights, and overconsumption.

In her testimony *Peggy Antrobus* (1991-3) says "If women are to clean up the mess they have a right to challenge the people and institutions which create the problems. To do this, they need to understand the links between environmental degradation and the structures of social,

33

economic and political power, and the links between policies and actions in far off places (...) and the conditions under which they live".

The final tribunal identified three major guiding principles, which are worked out in specific proposals. The first is global equity; priority should be given to basic human rights and needs, including a healthy and sustainable environment. The second is resource ethics; ethical principles are needed in order to balance the need for material progress with the sustainable use of resources, and to base living standards on long-term sustainability. The third principle is the empowerment of women; their perspective should be brought to bear on global problems of environmental destruction and poverty.

The final report also gives the edited version of "Women's Action Agenda 21" (an alternative to UNCED's "Agenda 21"), which links matters of democracy, ethics, debt and trade, poverty, land rights, food security, population policies, biodiversity and biotechnology, science and technology transfer, and consumption in revolutionary standpoints on what needs to be done to create a healthy planet. It also calls for a permanent, gender-balanced UN Commission on Environment and Development, to help create and watch over an International Code of Environmental Conduct. The recommendations are "a basic guide to women's efforts to promote environmental and economic security now and on into the 21st century".

Also very worthwhile are the statements and action plans that came out of the regional and special caucuses, reflecting both agreement among women of different backgrounds, and their differences in terms of problems and priorities. Some examples. The European women committed themselves to use their consumer power to change consumption and production patterns and to search for "people and nature respecting" economics. The African women elaborated on alternatives to structural adjustment and demanded against militarization. The indigenous women urged the world to follow a long-term ethic based upon the "laws of the natural world that govern creation". The Latin American and Caribbean caucus report (in Spanish) is strongly anti-imperialist (for example on "debt-for-nature-swaps"[6]) and insists on the recognition of the ecological debt of the developed countries, and women's reproductive rights. The decision on Women in Environment and Development as adopted by *UNCED Prepcom III* (1991-1) is given in full (see also 1.3).

34

The extensive document resulting from the Global Forum, the NGO parallel conference during UNCED, contains alternative treaties on subjects discussed at UNCED -and important ones which were left undiscussed in the official conference. The Women's Treaty mainly builds on "Women's Action Agenda 21" *(Pollard et al.* 1992).

2.3 Readers and special issues

Other possibilities to begin with are the readers compiled by *Ellen Sprenger* (1991, University of Nijmegen), *Loes Schenk-Sandbergen* (1991-1/2, University of Amsterdam), *ISIS International* (1991), and *Sally Sontheimer* (1991). *Schenk-Sandbergen* collected articles with special emphasis on the urban context in India, for the purpose of an introductory lecture series on women, ecology and development. The article of *Bina Agarwal* (1989), is especially worth mentioning, since she elaborates on what Vandana Shiva leaves undiscussed: the traditional inequalities in India, such as intrahousehold differences in distribution of basic necessities and women's disadvantaged labour position. She argues that women's militancy in grassroots resistance is much more linked to family survival, and connected with social and cultural improvement than men's ("their struggle is not just for bread, but also for dignity"). Their militancy is also an implicit attempt to create an alternative existence, based on equality and cooperation. *Sprenger's* reader includes some interesting contributions on ecofeminism, the "nature-culture" debate and feminist theory. *ISIS International's* information package contains loose and mostly short materials from different angles, which makes it widely useable. The reader compiled and introduced by *Sontheimer* contains five articles of prominent writers *(Moser, Dankelman and Davidson,* etc.).

For a quick glance at the subject some of the numerous "special issues on women and environment" are worth mentioning, such as the issue of the magazine *Earthwatch,* with a good introductory contribution from Davidson (1989). The special issue of *the Ecologist* (1992) goes into theoretical issues, and an issue of the *Wanawake* (1991) contains some interesting interviews. Furthermore, there is an issue of *Women and Environments* (1991), dealing with Northern consumer issues (e.g. *Bernadette Vallely)* and Southern problems *(Rosemary Brown)* both. For the urban context, the special issue of *Environment and Urbanization* (1991) on gender is a good introduction.

In the above-mentioned writings, the relation between women, environment and development is evident, but still the roots of environmental and gender problems in development are often left uncovered; the question of how gender ideology and other factors have been influential in GED is mostly left undiscussed. The next two chapters are meant to provide some stepping stones across the wide river of literature on these issues.

Notes

1 *Arts and van Reisen* refer to *Redclift* (1987) for a complementary structural analysis. In a later paper by Dankelman (1991) the macrolevel consequences for sustainable development are better indicated (see further macrocontext chapter 3)

2 In particular in relation to the biological sciences there is an ongoing – sometimes fierce – debate about the value of a holistic versus reductionist approach of biological processes. Those in favour of holism, consider biological systems to be more than the sum of the parts. "Reductionists" assume that ecosystems can be understood on the basis of the analysis of the functioning of its parts, reducing biological phenomenons to physical-chemical processes. Evidently, these approaches lead to different kinds of research methods and have led to different "schools", for instance in the ecological sciences. However, both approaches within the ecological sciences still consider ecosystems in isolation. With a few exceptions, socio-political, cultural and other human factors are not taken into consideration.

3 Ecofeminism is a philosophical strand, and will be dealt with 3.3.

4 For example at the *Global Assembly* (1991), Aloisi de Larderel (UNEP) gave a rather technocratic view on cleaner production. Capeling-Alakija (UNIFEM), still emphasised the "integration" of women in development. Tovo (ESMAP, Worldbank) talking about energy proposed a "holistic approach" but this does not go beyond the improved woodstove, a very outdated and still reductionist view on the issue of energy (see e.g. *Groen* 1989).

5 These tapes are in the InDRA collection.

6 Debt-for-nature-swaps implies that a country or institution "buys" a part of the foreign debt of a country. This money is used to protect an interesting piece of nature in the indebted country. This activity is often seen as just another form of neo-colonialism.

CHAPTER 3

Theoretical approaches to gender, environment and development

It is easy to fall into the trap of making a strict distinction between theory and practice, as if it concerned two different worlds.[1] This causes developmental agencies to "deal with practical problems first" without being aware of the framework of ideas in which they are working. It causes scientists to elaborate on theory without taking into account the ideas of the people they theorize about. It is important to recognize the dominant ideas that have influenced academics and development agencies in dealing with GED. It is worthwile to take notice of theories in which these dominant ideas are unmasked and alternatives formulated. These alternative theories are often derived from practical experiences "in the field".

An extensive mapping of influential ideas in the debate on women, environment and development was made by *Sabine Haüsler and Ewa Charkiewicz-Pluta* (1991-1, extended and published see *Braidotti et al.* 1993). Theirs is a state-of-the-art report on perspectives on WED, derived from the development, the ecological and the feminist movements. It is an attempt to explore the theoretical connections between different criticisms of development, and a proposal to combine the different theories in an alternative framework. In their view each of these different perspectives has useful contributions to make to the "transformative momentum" of development. They discuss concepts such as developmentalism, WID (women in development) WED (women, environment and development), environmental reformism, deep and social ecology, ecofeminism, feminist critique of science and development, and the ideas of DAWN. I refer to this book for those interested in a more extensive description of influential ideas than can be given in this guide.

As discussed in chapter 1, the fields of "women and development" and "environment and development" have developed rather independently in policy and planning, and so did the theorizing about both fields. There is no substantial analytical work on the different approaches to

GED in policy and planning yet. However, the interconnection of GED is dealt with in quite a few philosophical writings.

Although general development theory has greatly influenced the way in which "women and development" and "environment and development" have been conceptualized, I do not deal seperately with this general theory. In the issues discussed below, much of the general development debate can be found back.

In the first paragraph of this chapter I discuss different approaches in the field of women and gender and development. Three major approaches are highlighted, which may well be relevant for dealing with the environmental issue from a gender point of view: "gender planning", "autonomy" and the ideas of the Southern women's network called DAWN. In the second paragraph, I briefly discuss some approaches to environment and sustainable development, both in policy and in philosophical writings. Followed in the third paragraph by an extensive discussion on a remarkable strand in philosophy: "ecofeminism". Feminist critiques of science are mentioned in connection.

Ideas about gender and environment as reflected in policy documents are dealt with seperately in chapter 6.

3.1 Approaches to women, gender and development

There is an overwhelming amount of literature on the issue of women, gender and development. *VENA* (et al. 1992) have compiled a short, but informative reader (all in English) for one of their courses, which is a good starting point for reading. It links theory with the issue of planning. An extensive book which does the same, and gives many case-studies is edited by *Tina Wallace and Candida March* (1991). It includes case-studies on the impact of the global crisis on women, barriers to women's development, and working with gender issues. One chapter of it appears in a reader from the Dutch *Royal Tropical Institute* (1991), which contains many other interesting references (note also their bibliography 1993). An introduction of why gender is to be preferred above women and development is to be found in *CCIC et al.* (1992) a handbook for gender analysis and programming. *Irene Tinker* (1990) has edited a book which provides a historical and political overview of the field of women in economic development and some major areas of current research.

The approaches which I chose to deal with more in detail in this section are "gender planning", "autonomy" and the Third World feminist ideas of DAWN. These three may be called important approaches in the field of gender and development nowadays. Before going into them, it may be useful to show the different approaches which have ruled policies towards women in the South.

The development of approaches
A well-known introduction to the issue of women and gender in development, is written by *Caroline Moser* (1989-1).[2] She describes and reviews the following policy approaches to "Women In Development"[3], a "classification" which is often referred to:

1 The "welfare approach", of the '50s and '60s, was based on the Western stereotype that women's work was restricted to the reproductive sphere. Women were perceived as victims of underdevelopment, an idea which led to top-down handouts of goods and services.

2 The "equity approach" came up in the early '70s (inspired by *Boserup* 1970). The UN Decade for Women ('75-'85) endorsed this approach, which lacks an analysis of gender/power structures.

3 The "anti-poverty " approach of the '70s focused on basic needs, and on women's productive roles.

4 The "efficiency" approach which came up in the late '70s, is also called the instrumental approach, because it sees women as human resource for development.[4]

5 The "empowerment" approach, the latest, has been inspired by Southern women. Historically based inequalities have to be broken by strengthening and extending the power base of women.

Using Moser's classification, the approaches of gender planning, autonomy and the ideas of DAWN would all fall under "empowerment". However, these approaches are all quite different, as will be discussed.

Noeleen Heyzer (1991) has made another historical overview of approaches, also starting with the "welfare approach". Then, she classifies approaches 2, 3 and 4 as given by *Moser* all under the heading "integration approach".

The idea of the integration approach is that women should have a fair share in the benefits of development. This approach has been hard to change, although it is widely criticized (e.g. *Geertje Lycklama a Nijeholt* (1987), *Joke Schrijvers* (1985), *Els Postel* (1990)). The core of criticism is that the direction of the development in which women should integrate or participate is not questioned. Women should be able to choose their own direction of development instead.

After the integration approach, Heyzer mentions the emergence of "gender sensitive planning and implementation" (the idea put forward by *Moser* herself, see below), in which realities of women's lives are considered in the planning and implementation of development programmes.

Seperately, she mentions the "empowerment approach", building on women's capacities to overcome the pressures and problems of poverty and gender inequity. *Heyzer* states that gender sensitive planning and empowerment are both needed to reduce poverty and to promote gender equity. In fact this implies a combination of a top-down and bottom-up approach. I will come back to this later.

Gender planning, practical and strategic gender needs
Caroline Moser has been a leading person in the gender and development circles, outlining the gender planning perspective (1989-1 a.o.). Looking from this perspective means reviewing development projects according to the degree of recognition of the triple role of women, and reviewing which practical or strategic gender needs these projects meet. The triple role of women refers to their roles in reproduction, production and community management/politics. *(Wendy Harcourt* (1991-1) adds another role to this triple role of women: natural resource management!)

Practical gender needs are formulated from actual conditions in women's engendered position (e.g. improved cooking stoves). Addressing these needs means helping women to carry out their tasks without addressing their problematic position. Strategic gender needs are formulated from the analysis of women's subordination by men (e.g. abolition of a sexual division of labour). Addressing these needs would contribute to more gender equality.[5]

Hilda Bonsink (1989) summarizes some critics of the rather artificial distinction between these practical and strategic gender needs, but concludes that the distinction is useful especially to guarantee that the strategic needs are not neglected *(Bonsink* 1989). The distinction may however be misleading. Southern women's needs are easily seen by development agencies as primarily practical. However, what may seem practical gender needs for outsiders may have strategic potential as well for the women involved. For example, learning to ride a bicycle may be a practical improvement, but it also implies greater mobility and independence. Conversely, the tradition of "dealing with practical problems first", may be reinforced by this distinction. "First the practical needs, then the strategic" is an idea which does not work, because they cannot be separated. A classical example is the use of improved woodstoves, which by itself neither solves environmental degradation, nor women's own "energy crisis" (their extra heavy workload caused by their problematic position).

One could speak of a "Moser school" of gender planning, in fact a kind of reformist approach to the established development traditions, which is easily used top-down.[6] Since the late '80s gender training for development experts, often based on her work, has become institutionalized. But, *Wendy Harcourt* states (1991-1)"Gender and development remains a largely marginalized field analytically and in practice. (.....) Women's present situation in developing countries should be met by gender strategic needs which take into account the need to raise women's social and economic status, their self-determination, and men's supportive awareness".

Gender planning does not question the assumptions of the dominant development paradigm. Furthermore, its efficiency is entirely dependent on the goodwill of governments and their willingness to allow women's equity.
CCIC et al. in their gender manual, however, outline an approach which claims to alter this dominant development paradigm. They explain: "Gender And Development is emerging as a progressive approach to development from women's perspectives and experiences (...). It is part of the larger work of creating an alternative development model, for a world view which moves beyond an economistic analysis to include environmental, sustainable and qualitative (personal, ethical and cultural) aspects in its definition of development" *(CCIC et al.* 1991). Still, it is crucial how this idea is worked out in a methodology.

Autonomy
The "autonomy" concept may also be useful to oppose the above-mentioned critique of consolidating the assumptions of the

dominant development paradigm, although the concept is prone to misuse. The Dutch Ministry of Foreign Affairs has adopted the concept as formulated by *Joke Schrijvers* (e.g. 1985, esp. 1991).

The concept has been adapted from ideas formulated by South Asian women. It refers to a situation of self-determination, and may be summarized as: control over one's own body and life, which has physical, economic, political and ideological dimensions. It may be interesting at this point, to outline why all four elements of this concept are relevant for the environmental issue. The physical aspect of autonomy is directly threatened when family planning for "environmental policy reasons" endangers women's reproductive rights, and when pollution and radiation effects are leading to e.g. miscarriages. Autonomy in the economic sphere includes access and control over resources, crucial for women's environmental management possibilities. The political element includes environmental policy making, and women's participation in working towards sustainable development in general. The ideological (or socio-cultural) dimension, including a positive self-image is crucial for the countervailing power which women have to exert to gain more control over their environment (including access to resources, opposing pollution, etc). It must be stressed, however, that the elements of autonomy are closely linked and cannot be dealt with in isolation, just like the natural environment cannot be dealt with in isolation from the political, economic, social environment, etcetera.

The autonomy approach goes even further than the empowerment approach because it springs from a bottom-up view on socio-political transformation. Empowerment (sometimes perceived as "to give power to somebody else", see *Schrijvers* 1991) may still have the top-down character which is rejected in the autonomy concept. So, autonomy has met a lot of resistance from development experts, also because it conflicts with the ideal of women's self-sacrifice and altruism *(Schrijvers* 1991). Despite this resistance autonomy has become a key concept for women in the Dutch parliamentary development policy document *(Tweede Kamer* 1990), and should be an integral part of this policy. In a speech, *Jan Pronk,* as the Dutch Minister of Development Cooperation, has outlined the autonomy concept as it is adopted, and summarized the critiques. Autonomy, according to the critics, is individualistic, not relational, not based on gender and typically Western. He opposes the critiques and sketches the applicability of the concept *(Jan Pronk,* 1991). *Schrijvers* again mentions the risks of this "appropriation" of the concept by Dutch policy; "it may be used as mechanistic, instrumental and superficial device to measure things that can't be measured" *(Schrijvers 1993)*.

Autonomy as interpreted by Southern women activists is often seen as the necessary space for women and men to be able to work towards a different society, in which democracy, peace and social justice rule. And thus autonomy can apply to groups as well. The criticisms mentioned above, e.g. that the striving towards autonomy is promoting individualism, may be called projections of typically Western thought on communities in the South.

The ideas of DAWN
Many Southern feminists have criticized the concept of development emerging from science. *Kumar d'Soeza* (1991) "In the name of universalism the west exported its theoretical models, its development and its science, its wars and its weapons to the Third World, colonizing its economies, determining its political processes, stifling its cultures, siliencing its civilizations".

Especially noteworthy in this respect is the DAWN network (Development Alternatives with Women for a New Era). The group was formed by active Southern women at the end of the Women's Decade (1975-1985), to consider what could be learned from that experience.

"Development, crisis and alternative visions: Third World women's perspectives" *(Sen and Grown* 1985/87), gives an overview of their analysis. Like *Shiva's* book (1989) it is a clear argument for the reassessment of the ideas behind development strategies from Third World women's views, experiences and actions, with which DAWN wants to arrive at a new development paradigm. Gender is linked with a general crisis of sustainability: "A development process that shrinks and poisons the pie available to poor people, and then leaves women scrambling for a larger relative share, is not in women's interest". DAWN coordinator *Peggy Antrobus* more recently (e.g.1991-1/1992) described the ideas of DAWN.

Reviewing the Women's Decade, a feminist critique of growth-oriented development has emerged, and an analytical link between various crises. DAWN interlinks the crises of debt, poverty, food shortage, environmental degradation, militarization, political conservatism and religious fundamentalism. DAWN envisions a world in which "inequality based on class, gender and race is absent from every country, and from the relationships among countries". Their perspective aims to be holistic; linking social, economic, cultural, political and environmental factors. It is grounded in an alternative paradigm of social change, it is political, feminist, and attempts to link household level experiences of poor women to macroeconomic policies. DAWN promotes a "people centred" approach, equitable development based on cooperation, resistance to hierarchies, sharing, accountability and commitment to peace. The use of natural resources is placed in a political perspective *(Antrobus* 1989, 1991-1, see also *Haüsler and Pluta* 1991-1). DAWN's analysis has broadened and deepened the debate on gender and development.[7]

3.2 Approaches to environment and sustainable development

As discussed in the introduction, since the early '70s the environment has slowly, or in fact in shocks, become an issue in international development policy. The international community seems to have become aware of the relations between development, poverty and environmental degradation. "Sustainable development" has been put forward as a global problem solving strategy, a process to be chanelled through international and national institutions. Others interpret sustainable development more as a shift to local self-reliance, with empowerment of the poor or ecology as the main guiding principles. A sketch of the spectrum.

Sustainable development
Although the concept was not totally new, the idea of sustainable development was given a strong impulse by the Brundtland report *(WCED* 1987). Their definition of sustainable development is the most frequently quoted in the literature: "development that meets the needs of the present generations without compromising the ability of future generations to meet their own needs" (WCED 1987). Since then, this concept has ruled many discussions. Besides an economic dimension, sustainable development also has ecological, social and political dimensions.[8] It encompasses the problematics of degradation of natural resources, the development of the Third World, and the international social and political relations *(Arts and Berghuizen* 1992). However, economic growth remains as the core, seen as a necessity to environmental protection. There is no agreement on this point, states *Diana Mitlin* (1992),who has written a short guide to the literature on

sustainable development. She states that most writers from the North focus on "sustainability": rather than sustainable development, exploring how present environmental constraints may be overcome and the standards of living maintained, while the social dimension is often ignored (The Brundtland report is an example).[9]

There is also little agreement on the causes of the present lack of sustainability, she states, and little analysis of the present lack of commitment on the part of governments and individuals. *Mitlin* discusses definitions and approaches to sustainable development found in literature, and texts with policy recommendations (about 50 references in total).

Mitlin however pays little attention to the fact that the concept of sustainable development itself and the misuse of the concept have been much criticized. To begin with a Southern critic, *S.M. Mohamed Idris* (1990), who sketches what the Southern consequences of the Northern development model are. He states: "the term sustainable from the ecological point of view means maintenance of the integrity of the ecology. (...) The term sustainable from the point of view of non-ecological elites means how to continue to sustain the supply of raw materials when existing sources of raw materials run out". His article appeared in *Frijns/Hazeu* (1991), a useful introductory reader on environment and development. *Edward Goldsmith* (1988) puts: "Rural development, eco-development, sustainable development (...) are all euphemisms adopted by the development industry to placate its critiques". *Lezak Shallat* (1990) proposes the term "sustainable survival", for "what exactly is it that should be developed? Sustainable development of the environment makes little sense".

In fact, sustainable development is first a scientific concept, an interdisciplinary field of study, and second a normative concept including environmental ethics. Third, it is a political programme, which is not easily operationalized, because of the ideological oppositions that remain evident under the "common flag" of sustainable development (summarized by *Arts en Berghuizen* 1992).

Sustainable development and political economy
Bill Adams has written an extensive critique on the concept of sustainable development. In his well documented book (1990) he analyses the evolution of the concept, and its application in reality. He critically investigates development (economic development, development assistance) and its environmental consequences and states

that a part of the limitation of sustainable development thinking lies in its failure to address political economy[10]. Development and conservation both are dominated by global concentrations of wealth and power, and centralized decision-making. "Greening development involves not just a pursuit of ecological guidelines and new planning structures, but an attempt to redirect change to maintain or enhance the power of the poor to survive without hindrance and to direct their own lives". The concept of sustainable development does not have a coherent theoretical core, and its popularity is rather caused by its vagueness than by its strength. His book may serve as a thorough introduction to sustainable development, as does *Michael Redclift's* book (1987). *Redclift* pays some attention to the issue of women, which Adams does not.[11] Both discuss the relationship of socialism and capitalism with the environment, concluding that either system is unsuitable for sustainability. *Piers Blaikie and Harold Brookfield* (1987) use a "regional political ecology" approach[12] for their explanation of land degradation, with a primary emphasis on social and economic causes. For example, on the issue of population and land degradation they state that high population pressure never is a cause of environmental deterioration in itself, although it may create stress. It is rather an economic and political marginalization of people, combined with the marginalization of their natural environment in a downward spiral.[13]

Suzanna Hecht and Alexander Cockburn (1989/90) in "The fate of the forest" also examine sustainable development from a historical and political perspective and pay attention to the relevance of environmental theories.

Conroy and Litvinov (1988) have edited a book with 30 case-studies, directly or indirectly dealing with aid and sustainable development, and aiming to help development agencies promote sustainable development in their projects. It contains an inspiring introduction by *Robert Chambers* (1988), elaborating on "sustainable livelihood security" of the poor, an outline of a bottom-up approach. It starts from the point of view that poverty is a major cause of environmental degradation, and that the poor have the potential to operationalize a long-term perspective which the environment needs. He (in all his work) focuses on the local situation, without addressing international structures. *Redclift* (1987, see also *Goodman and Redclift* 1991), for example, does incorporate these structures, as do *Adams* (1990) and *Blaikie and Brookfield* (1987).

Deep Ecology
Michael Colby (1989) has written an overview of the evolution of
paradigms in environmental management in development. He describes
the concepts of "frontier economics", "deep ecology", "environmental
protection", "resource management" and "ecodevelopment". He
discusses their distinctions, connections and their implications for future
environmental management in development. Deep ecology as a concept
in fact opposes "environmental management", because it refers, in short
to a critique of "antropocentrism", the idea that human beings are the
masters of the world. It promotes "biocentrism"(e.g. *Arne Naess*
1989/90). Deep ecology criticizes the more reformist ideas that solutions
to environmental problems can be found within the existing
technocratic growth model (like appropriate technologies, better
management etc). Deep ecologists have in turn been accused of
neglecting social and cultural analyses of the roots of the ecological
crisis, especially its gender dimension (see e.g. *Michael Zimmerman* 1987).

Writings on deep ecology and other ecophilosophical strands can be
found in an annotated bibliography compiled by *Donald Edward Davis*
(1989). The magazines *Environmental Ethics* and *the Ecologist*[14] have
published a series of articles on environmental philosophy, including the
concept of "ecofeminism" discussed below. Deep ecology and
ecofeminism both emphasize the unity of object/subject (in science),
and between nature and culture, and that the richness and diversity of
life are values in themselves (*Deval & Session* 1985). Ecofeminists and
Southern development critics have however contributed to a social,
cultural and women's perspective that deep ecology has been lacking.[15]

3.3 Ecofeminism and critique of science

Ecofeminism may be the most prominent approach to the GED debate.
In fact, different factions of feminisms, Southern critiques on them,
spirituality and the ecology movement come together in this concept
(*King* 1989). According to *Ynestra King,* (and many others) ecofeminism
is not just an intellectual project, it is linked with direct survival
struggles. Karen Warren (1987) has written a clear article on
ecofeminism. She states that ideas within ecofeminism do vary, but that
the concept is based on the following claims:

1 There are connections between the oppression of nature and the oppression of women.
2 Understanding these connections is necessary to understand the oppression of both.
3 Feminist theory must include an ecological perspective.
4 Solutions to ecological problems must include a feminist perspective.
Important in ecofeminism is the rejection of normative dualism (discussed below), and its replacement by interconnectedness, equality, and diversity. These principles become clearer as one examines the first feature of the ecofeminist approach which is the recognition of the historical connection between the oppression of both women and nature.

Simultaneous oppression of women and nature
Many writers have elaborated on this theme. For anyone interested in the women and nature debate, and a feminist critique of science *Carolyn Merchant's* book "The Death of Nature; Women, Ecology and the Scientific Revolution" is a must (1980 etc, note also 1992). She inspired many later writers with this extensive exploration of the historical association of women with nature. The ancient identification of nature with a "nurturing mother" (in many cultures) links women's history with the history of the environment and environmental change. Under the influence of e.g. Descartes, and Bacon, and for the sake of the industrial revolution, ideas about the universe were transformed in the 16th and 17th century from thinking of the world as a living organism to thinking of it as an inanimate object, or a machine. This dominant mechanistic worldview[16] has sanctioned the domination of both women and nature, because women have been closely associated with nature. In her foreword anno 1990 *Merchant* states that the mechanistic unilineair models in natural science have now been abandoned, but new models should be worked out and combined with an ecological ethic. *Hans Achterhuis* (1990), on a similar track, vividly describes the roots of the humanist idea that man (or men) can master nature, the idea that both women and nature are to be tamed by force; conquered and improved by subjection. He quotes Bacon on the goal of science: "force nature to serve you and make her your slave". *Achterhuis* states that the world has been transferred from "Mother Earth" to a "Spaceship", directed by man. On this spaceship the focus is on the environment rather than on nature, and on human survival rather than on a possible good life. This spaceship idea is found back in many recent writings on environment and development (like the Brundtland report, *WCED* 1987).

Rosemary Brown (1991) argues that the simultaneous oppression of women and nature still goes on, because (after the colonial period) "development" shrouded in the rhetoric of aid, assistance and caring, has really been the "bridge" which allowed exploitation of Third World women (as cheap labour) and the environment (by pillaging resources) to proceed unchecked (Brown 1991). The sexual division of labour is often recognized as a mode of oppression related to the women and nature connection. *Maria Mies* (1988), states that it is not crucial to understand the origins of the division itself, but rather to understand the reasons why this division became assymetric, hierarchical and exploitative. Inspired by marxism, she links gender and environment with class struggles, arguing that women's bodies and nature were "colonized" by patriarchy and capitalism in combination *(Mies* 1986, note also *Mies and Shiva* 1993).

 Gabrielle Dietrich links the ecological crisis with a cultural crisis, referring to the class and caste struggles in India. She points at the industrial mode of development which assaults the base for human material and spiritual survival (1988-2). According to *Dietrich* one of the causes of ecological degradation is the sexual division of labour, because it has kept women out of science and technology. She suggests a "New Science of Life", in which women would be the basis and the leaders (1989).

The oppression of women and nature is also elaborated upon by feminist critics of science like *Donna Haraway* (1989 and 1991), *Evelyn Fox Keller* (1985), *Sandra Harding* (1986, 1991) and *Vandana Shiva* 1988-2, 1989, 1991-I see 2.1). Important other feminist critics of science are *Nancy Tuana* (1989),and *Lynda Birke* (biology, 1986).

 Christien Brouwer (1990) explores a possible feminist view on the relation scientist/nature. *Brouwer et al.* (1992) have made a succinct bibliography containing more references on this subject. Other references on the connection of GED to science are given in an extensive bibliography on feminist views at science and technology *(Eldredge* 1990). Also, many references to feminist critiques of science occur in an extensive bibliography on ecofeminism and related subjects *(Jansen* 1990).

Beyond normative dualism
Karen Warren, in the above-mentioned article (1987) stated that the connection between the oppression of both women and nature lies in

the conceptual framework of patriarchal thinking, which gives rise to a logic of domination of what has been identified as male over what has been identified as female. This implies a normative dualism, dividing the world in two opposites and valuing one over the other: men over women, human over non-human, etc. This kind of dualist thinking, oppressive of both women and nature[17], is opposed by the ecological principles of interconnectedness, equality and diversity, which are therefore also fundamental for ecofeminism. *Ynestra King*, states that women also have a bridging function between nature and culture, because their activities like mothering, healing, farming are as social as they are natural. The recognition of the historical bond between women and nature, and women's bridging function between culture and nature, can result in three ways of thinking. The first is to break the bond, often perceived as a prerequisite for the liberation of women. Feminists, she argues, are understandably wary of any theory that appears to reinforce the women/nature relationship as biological determinism by another name. At the same time ecologists have been demonstrating the perilous situation of life on earth brought about by human attempts to master nature. This has led other feminists to assert that the feminist project should be freeing nature from men rather than freeing women from nature. Thus, the second way of thinking is to cherish and strengthen the bond between women and nature: women as saviours of the earth.[18] The third way of thinking is to start from the historical bond between women and nature in order to define a political strategy to create another culture and politics *(King,* 1983-1/1990). This third approach is a "social" ecofeminist approach (see next paragraph), recognizing that all humans act in a socially constructed framework, influenced by gender, race, class, age, sexual preference, religion and nationality.

Cultural and social ecofeminism
In the literature there is much confusion about ecofemism because writers often stick to connecting "women and nature", without a social and historical analysis, and argue for either breaking or cherishing the bond between women and nature. Examples of more biologistic views on the bond between women and nature are seen, for instance Suzan Griffin in *Caldecott and Leyland* (1983): "Those of us who are born female are often less severely alienated from nature than most men". Other examples form *Collard and Contrucci* (1988), and several contributions in *Diamond and Orenstein* (1990). *Melissa Leach* (1991-1) states that ecofeminism is simply invalid as a cross-cultural project,

risking to impose ideas about female nurturance of natural resources. Furthermore, she argues, ecofeminism gives women the sole responsibility for saving the environment with no attention to whether or not they have the resources to do so *(Leach* 1991-1). However, she only criticizes a concept of ecofeminism which *Val Plumwood* (1992) calls "cultural ecofeminism". "Cultural ecofeminism" stresses the link between women and nature, reducing all forms of oppression to the oppression of women. *Susan Prentice* (1988) also criticizes only the concept of "cultural ecofeminism", when she argues that ecofeminism reinforces gender. Ecofeminism, she says, causes trivialization of socio-political factors, and has a "reactionary" idealism: it would set the women's movement back. Cultural ecofeminism, however, does not fit into the characteristics of ecofeminism outlined above (the rejection of dualism, the recognition of history and social processes determining women's relation to nature), and is less suitable in a theoretical framework of gender and environment. The ecofeminist strand which was outlined before could be called "social ecofeminism" *(Plumwood* 1992), emphasizing the social and political aspects of gender and environment, considering gender as a dimension of power together with race, class, caste etc.

Warren (1987) and *King* (1989) both describe why various leading factions of feminism are unsuitable as basis for (social) ecofeminism. They argue that all capitulate to dualism (e.g. men/women, nature/culture) or natural determinism (e.g. women are closer to nature than men). *Haüsler and Charkiewicz-Pluta* (1991-1) in their chapter on ecofeminism summarize their arguments.

Compilations of ecofeminist ideas
Ecofeminism is both a philosophical and a political approach. Although the term is Northern, its principles are often worked out in "survival based feminism of women of color, emerging from their experience at the crucible of multiple oppressions" (quoted from *King* 1989, who uses the expression in a different context). The report of the *World Women's Congress* (1992) based on grass roots experiences and geared towards policy change, also reflects many of the ideas described above (see also chapter 8).
Judith Plant has edited a book (1989) with contributions of some prominent writers. *Kumar D'Soeza* (e.g. in this work and 1991), combines ecofeminist with socialist ideas, and speaks from "The Wind

from the South", urging for more respect of the plurality of different cultures and traditions.

A more extensive and up to date bundle of ecofeminist contributions is by *Diamond and Orenstein* (1990). This could be a good starting point for reading, besides *Warren* (1987). The collection of articles, essays and poetic prose show a coming together of the environmental, feminist and spirituality movements. In this work, *Ynestra King* explains the nature/culture dualism; *Carolyn Merchant* draws a chart of different kinds of feminisms and their attitude towards nature, human nature and environmentalism; *Judith Plant* connects ecofeminism with bioregionalism, the idea that humans should fit themselves to a particular place rather than fitting a place to their tastes (See also *Andruss et al.* 1990); *Susan Griffin* puts more emphasis on gender in her article here than in her earlier publications (in Caldecott and Leyland 1983, 1978/80).

Connections with other philosophical strands
It may be interesting to see how philosophical ideas such as deep ecology and (eco)feminism can be interlinked, also with Southern ecology and development movements (see e.g. *Zimmerman* 1987, *Johns* 1990, *de la Court* 1991).

Bookchin (1990), representing the "social ecology" concept, argues that it is necessary to "improve the project of modernity, revive the ideals of emancipation and unite social movements (feminist, ecology, consumer, solidarity and Third World development movement) around the issue of ecology, survival of Earth and human livelihood". In fact, this process has been taking place since the early '90s. The NGO parallel conference to UNCED, the "Global Forum", has been able to unite different movements in an action plan to save the environment. Of course it remains to be seen what will be achieved. It is anyway clear that an attempt is made in philosophy and NGO circles to link ecological, feminist and (other) Southern points of view. We may expect more work on suitable theoretical frameworks for dealing with gender and environment in sustainable development in the near future.

Most of the above-mentioned critics have discussed dominant development processes and their impact on gender and the way of dealing with the natural environment. The ideology which has been criticized, the ideology of the western, white male as "knower", and ruler of a makeable world often lies at the basis of the policies and processes in the wider context of gender, environment and development, as discussed in the next chapter.

Notes

1 I do not mean the distinction between rhetoric and practice, (which should instead be critically reviewed in dealing with GED!), but between theoretizing on the one hand and practical development work on the other. Development workers may see the latter as "reality" and the first as "only theory". Theorists may see practical development work through existing development channels as a "marginal effort", because more fundamental changes are needed. Both perceptions keep the gap between theory and practice wide open.

2 This article appears in three of the introductory references mentioned above. It outlines the gender planning perspective, dealt with below.

3 "Women In Development" is the terminology of USAID. The term has different underlying assumptions, and is therefore unclear. One of their publications is dealt with in chapter 7, in which these assumptions are discussed (USAID 1989). The shift of approaches as outlined by Moser concerns US development cooperation, but it also applies to many other development institutions, including the Dutch government (see e.g. Pronk 1991).

4 This instrumental approach is clearly reflected in some documents dealt with in 6.1 and 7.2.

5 She bases this division on Molyneux (1987).

6 Noeleen Heyzer, as outlined above classified the ideas as described by Moser not under "empowerment". Moser, however, classifies her own ideas in fact under "empowerment", stating that from the gender planning perspective "empowerment" would be the best approach (1989-1). The gender planning perspective however remains top-down oriented. It implies that development institutions determine the direction of change, taking women "into consideration". Moser's approach does not question the existing power structures, or promote a different kind of development, and is as such "reformist".

7 For more on women/ gender and development the reader is referred to the VENA documentation centre in Leiden (the Netherlands) or other women's documentation centers. Literature lists on the subject are for instance given by the Dutch Ministry (1991), and the bibliography of the Royal Tropical Institute (1993).

8 Bhasin et al. (1991) explain the terms ecological sustainability, social sustainability, cultural sustainability and economic sustainability. The first aims to maintain ecological processes, biological diversity and resources. The second means maintaining peoples' control over their lives and well being. The third, cultural sustainability, demands development compatible with the

culture and values of the people. Economic sustainability requires efficiency and equity within and between generations. These elements are considered crucial to sustainable development.

9 See also previous footnote. Authors who use the term "social sustainability" either mean the social conditions of environmental sustainablity, or the sustainablity of a social system. The latter is problematic, *Mitlin* (1992) argues, because sustainable social systems can be the most exploitative regarding natural resources, and social systems are continuously changing. I must comment that sustainable does not necessarily mean stable, and that an exploitative social system in the long run is not sustainable, because the social system interacts with the natural system in a dynamic way. Social sustainablity thus cannot be separated from ecological sustainability, and ideally they should "coevoluate".

10 Political economy may be described as the theory in which economic, social and political power relations are considered central to the understanding of development processes at all levels (local to international).

11 His dealing with the women's issue is discussed by *Arts and van Reijsen* (1988) who compare the differences between *Redclift's* (1987) and *Dankelman and Davidson's* approach (1988))

12 In fact, the theory of political economy applied to ecology. Power relations are considered central to the understanding of environmental degradation on a regional scale.

13 The population issue is a hot issue in the GED debates, dealt with in 4.3.

14 Note e.g. *Edward Goldsmith* on the concept of "Gaia" in *The Ecologist*, vol 18 (2) and (4/5) (1988).

15 Note in this respect also *Bookchin* (1990), writing on the concept of "social ecology", arguing for an integration of different critical approaches to development.

16 Newton has been the father of mechanism in physics, but the idea had an earlier philosophical source.

17 This idea of similar oppression of women and nature is worked out in an example on biotechnology and reproductive technology in 4.4.

18 *Vandana Shiva* is often accused for doing this, see 2.1.

CHAPTER 4

Relevant global issues

Many worldwide environmental problems like overgrazing, deforestation, loss of biological diversity, loss of soil fertility, flooding, salinization, erosion, desertification and pollution are caused by processes at the international and national level, yet they have the greatest impact at the local level. As emphasized earlier, the problems are primarily felt by poor women, who are dependent on natural resources to perform their tasks to maintain livelihood (see *Rodda* 1991, *Dankelman and Davidson* 1988, *Dankelman* 1991 etc.)

There is an increasing recognition of the relationship between global, national, and regional policies and local processes with regard to GED. The testimonies given at the *World Women's Congress For a Healthy Planet* (1991-1/1992) for instance, reflect an upcoming emphasis on factors at the macrolevel.

It is important to chart the effects of the dominant development paradigm (cf chapter 3), as well as national and international policies and processes on gender and environment at the local level. Quite a few authors refer to the need to address macro- and mesolevel processes, but then continue to focus on consequences for the local, project level (e.g. *DAC/OECD* 1988). However, it is just as important to chart the consequences at the macrolevel of these local level practices and experiences. Empowerment of women to strengthen their environmental management is one such consequence. The Indian economist (and founder of DAWN) *Devaki Jain:* "Macroprocesses, structures and theories (...) are the key to change (not the micro-grassroot organization), and at the same time issue based movements like environment, women, workers are the key instruments for change(....)" (1991). The *Global Assembly* (1992-1/2) and the *World Women's Congress* (1992) outline a number of these consequences at the macrolevel (see 2.2).

The previous chapter sketched critiques of the dominant world view and its consequences for nature and women. In the literature on GED there are discussions of certain major causes of problems in environment and development, problems which may have mainly emerged out of the dominant development ideology. Literature can be found on macroeconomics, with special emphasis on gender-blind and/or environment-blind national income accounting (4.1) and the problem of debt and structural adjustment. Both of these issues have played a key role in the failure of economic development as well as sustainable development in the South (4.2). Population pressure is another issue. Often the growing number of people on earth is problematized and one speaks of "population explosion". In this guide, the population pressure on natural resources is related to overconsumption by Northern countries and Southern elites (4.3) Another issue is the impact of technology development. Special types of technology which could be seen as a recent example of the simultaneous oppression of women and nature as discussed in 3.3 are reproductive technology and biotechnology (4.4) An issue that is not yet very well covered in the literature, is that of war and militarism and its detrimental effects on women and the environment in combination (4.5). There is a considerable number of references on the issue of food security, which in fact combines all those issues. To understand food security the link between macro-, meso- and microlevel processes concerning gender and environment is crucial (4.6). Important issues like international policy on tariffs and trade, which have an enormeous impact on agriculture, are not seperately dealt with. Neither are religious fundamentalism, political conservatism or other large-scale political and cultural factors affecting GED, as I have not come accross enough specific literature on these subjects. The focus is on publications (few until now!) that help gain a better understanding of the relationships between the macro- and microlevel in the context of GED.

4.1 The macroeconomic model

The development of the world is ruled by a macroeconomic model based on an international division of labour and capital, in which Southern countries provide cheap labour and raw materials. It has the capitalist feature of "externalising costs" to the South, the poor, to the environment and to the future, while the benefits end up with the powerful. It has the Northern scientific feature of reductionism; it allows neglect of vital elements, of the very basis of sustainable development.

A great value is attached to national income accounting. One result of this accounting is the Gross National Product which is believed to be an indicator of economic development. The existence, concepts and calculations of national income accounting ultimately reflect the ideology of the makeable world in which the natural environment and women's work are unproductive resources without a value attached.

Ester Boserup (1970) was the first to introduce an analysis of women and international development into academic discourse. She showed that although women are major contributors to (rural) economies, their contributions are neither reflected in national statistics nor in planning and implementation of government projects. She described the process of polarization and hierarchization of men's and women's roles because of modernization. Her work was criticized for her "undue reliance on the modern perspective and the utopian view of pre-capitalist sexual equity" (Drake in *Buechner et al.* 1990), but she set the trend in reviewing the impact of capitalist and socialist pressures, and the inclusion of reproductive labour in research. The Forward Looking Strategies for the Advancement of Women *(UN* 1986), as a result of reviewing the UN decade, emphasize the contributions of women to agriculture, food production, reproduction and household activities. The deficient measurements of women's work were recognized. *Rinske van der Bij* (1991), however, states that macroeconomic policies and trends are still percieved as gender-neutral. For example in calculating the Gross National Product gender is not considered, and the survival tasks and reproductive labour are still not counted. Thus IMF/World Bank policies and international investment policies lack an analysis of the position of women and gender consequences of e.g. Structural Adjustment Policies. *Buechner et al.* (1990) state that in order to change policy making, data reflecting the costs of the political decisions failing to account for women and the environment are of great importance. A key priority would be to create a greater understanding of relationships at microlevel, of household systems, and incorporation of this information into policies and decision-making.

Alternative approaches
Some writers have tried to find alternative ways of calculating national income. For example, *Roefie Hueting et al.* (1992) outline a new methodology for the calculation of sustainable national income, including loss of environmental functions. The *Group of Green Economists* (1992) outline an "ecological economics", based on the flow of energy instead of money. A writer proposing a radically different way of dealing with (macro)economics is *Marilyn Waring* (1988). Her book

expresses anger about the stupidity of neglecting nature in economic decision-making, and she criticizes the often hopeless efforts to put a monetary value on natural resources. She gives an example. A forest can be viewed as an economic resource, as a socio-cultural amenity and as an ecosystem. These three dimensions would require quite different "measures". Neoclassical economics and national income accounting allow only one view of the world. The forest in this view is only an economic resource. Thus, national income accounting favours the monocrop forestry approach, which is mostly undesirable from a socio-cultural and ecological point of view.[1]

Margit Kennedy (in *Linggard & Moberg* 1990) makes a proposition for a new monetary system, based on qualitative, instead of quantitative growth. Hazel Henderson (in *Development* 1990: 3/4) proposes Country Future Indicators to correct Gross National Product accounting as a measurement of development. These include an account of the depletion of non-renewable resources, and the status of minorities, ethnic populations and women.

UNDP has put forward the Human Development Index, in addition to the narrow GNP, in which also such matters as education and health care are weighed. *Wendy Harcourt* (1991-1) makes an attempt to reconceptualize development away from economic development to human centred development, in which the environment and women both are accounted for. She proposes a Gender Index to be added to calculations of the Human Development Index, and to those ways of accounting proposed by "total economists" (aiming to balance economic growth and ecology). This because an analysis of social and environmental indicators as ways of measuring economic growth never quite addresses the implications of this analysis for women.

4.2 Debt and Structural Adjustment

Detrimental to both women's position and the environment in the South is the burden of debts and Structural Adjustment Programmes imposed by IMF and the World Bank as a prerequisite for further loans. Victoria Drake (in *Buechner et al.* 1990) sketches the history of women in economic development, and states that it was precisely macroeconomic factors such as debts, inadequate adjustment, protectionism and the failure to establish democratic economic relationships, that caused the failure of the UN decade for women.

Jeanne Vickers (1991) in her useful introductory book outlines the origins of the world economic crisis, and states that the heaviest burden of the crisis, even aggravated by Structural Adjustment Programmes, lays on poor women, who earn less, own less and control less. In summary, measures of Structural Adjustment have a negative impact on women's political, legal, cultural and social status, mainly because women are the poorest, and responsible for food production, household and caring. The Structural Adjustment measures imply cutbacks in health and child-care services, educational services, elimination of food subsidies, emphasis on export cropping, falling wages, higher prices and bad employment possiblities or conditions. Vickers poses the hypothesis that the social and gender inequality is not only aggravated by the crisis, but a major cause of it. Undervaluing or neglecting women's economic contributions has made that Structural Adjustment creates further obstacles to women's participation, instead of supporting them. In new adjustment policies "with a human face" this role is more acknowledged. For further references on women and the economic crisis, one can use the bibliography of *JUNIC/NGO* (1988-2), or *Ria van Neerbos* (1992).

Vickers failed to mention the impact of debt and adjustment on the environment and its consequences for women. *Annabel Rodda* (1991, published after Vickers in the same book series) mentions some environmental impacts of debt: deforestation for timber (for foreign exchange), pollution by mining and refining, land degradation by cash cropping (on marginal lands), and less money for conservation. *Susan George* (1992) has found strong positive correlations between high levels of indebtedness and environmental degradation, especially deforestation, and states that structural adjustment creates further stress on already fragile ecosystems. The "export-led growth" model on which the IMF and the World Bank insist is purely extractive, involving the mining rather than the management of resources, and let alone their conservation. For example the extraction of timber and the expansion of pasture lands for export are stimulated. The marginalized poor then add to the degradation. The sad thing is that the loans themselves financed such environmental destructive projects as mega-dams, nuclear power plants, huge industrial and agricultural estates, often causing disruption of cultures and health *(George* 1988 and 1992).

Literature that combines the effects of structural adjustment on women and the environment is scarce. It seems that we have to make the connection ourselves.

A document of *DAC/OECD* (1988), although focusing on the local level, reads: "Major policies concerned with structural adjustment (for example increased cash cropping, higher food prices and reduced spending on basic services) will directly and indirectly affect women's environmental interests and the way they are able to respond". *Briones* (1991) of the Freedom from Debt Coalition in the Philippines mentions the fact that the debt problem has devastating effects on women and environment in the Philippines (and elsewhere); this problem, she argues, is "worse than any natural disaster".

4.3 Overconsumption and population

Population growth is often labeled as an "environmental problem", but the idea that it is not so much the number of people but what they consume, what part of the "ecoscope" they use, is slowly getting accepted. As stated in the Brundtland report *(WCED* 1987) the industrialized countries together use 80-85% of the world's fossil energy and resources, with just a quarter of the world's population. Also in Southern countries environmental problems are often a matter of distribution rather than of population pressure. Except for the fallacy of the environmental argument in the population debate itself, the self-determination of (especially Southern) women is threatened by population policies claiming to protect the environment against overpopulation ("reduce their fertility to reduce deforestation", Tovo in *Global Assembly* 1991). It is widely accepted that technical solutions to the scarcity of resources are opted for, like family planning and enhancing food production, without critically examining the underlying assumptions and socio-political factors. *Irene van Staveren* (1992) demystifies ten myths on population. First there is the argument of Northern overconsumption, as mentioned above. Furthermore, environmental problems in the South that seem local (like erosion), can often be traced back to a Northern economic order that is increasingly penetrating the South (erosion can be caused by e.g. the use of unsuitable lands by marginalized farmers etc). Poverty and environmental degradation are linked by dominant economic structures *(van Staveren* 1992). Thus, a more important factor to consider when population pressure and environment are linked is the overexploitation of resources to satisfy the greed of the North. As *Ruth Bamela Engo-Tjeda* puts it in her testimony on the World Women's Congress (1991-2): "Depletion of natural resources and increasing environmental toxity are the by-products of societal excess (i.e. the lifestyle of affluent societies)". It is because of inequal access to and control over resources that more and more people have to cope with less and less fertile land and other resources. Thus, both poverty and excessive wealth are detrimental to the environment. This has been a hot debate in the UNCED process, but the necessity for the Northern countries to cut back on their lifestyles is now formally recognized. One of the principles of the "Declaration of Rio" *(UNCED* 1992-1) reflects, however vaguely, a trade-off between reducing overconsumption and the population. It states: "to achieve sustainable development and a higher quality of life for all people, States should reduce and eliminate unsustainable patterns of production and consumption and promote demographic policies". In fact it is a matter of inequal opportunities and means for "buying the carrying capacity" of other countries *(Pietronella van den Oever* 1991, see also alternative treaty in *Pollard et al.* 1992)

An activist on consumerism, trying to link macrolevel problems with (Northern) microlevel consumer attitude and behaviour is *Bernadette Vallely* from WEN (e.g. 1991). "We got fed up with being told that only Science or Politics can solve all these problems (like environmental ones). Women are making key consumer decisions but they are disempowered by thinking that the only choices they have are the choices that are in their supermarkets". She states that it is not only what products you buy, but being a green consumer is also to consume less. She and other writers from WEN link the use of bleached, disposable paper with environmental problems like pollution and deforestation *(Costello et al.* 1989, see also *Armstrong and Scott* 1992) *Maria Mies* (1991) sketches a possible feminist consumer liberation movement, urging the shift to other than material satisfyers of human needs in Northern countries, a "moral economy" which would be decentralized, and a changed sexual division of labour.

Incentives
Besides the argument of Northern overconsumption and the world economic order, other arguments are found to pervert the environmental argument as a rationale to start family planning programmes. Some writers argue instead, that environmental degradation leads to heavier workloads for women, who need more children to help them! *(Joekes* 1989, *Dankelman* 1991-1) *Lappé and Collins* (1986/88) who unmask 12 myths on world hunger in their book, conclude: "The very changes necessary to end hunger: the

democratization of economic life, especially the empowerment of women, are key to reducing birth rates, so that the human population can come into balance with the rest of the natural world". However, as *Susan Joekes* (1989) puts it, countries easily opt for population control, because the ultimate causes of unsustainable development are so difficult to address. Evidence shows that the position of women is indeed of crucial influence in bringing down family size. Joekes argues that special women's programmes contribute to sustainable development (also) because they modify the incentives for bearing children, and as such are the main instrument for reducing fertility (see also 6.1). Still, these arguments only serve the position that population in the South should be reduced. *Jyotsna Gupta* (1991) indicates that the North makes use of (very expensive) reproductive technology to enhance fertility, while preaching birth control in Southern countries. In her testimony *Vanaja Ramprasad* (1991) links the above mentioned issues with women's health. For discussions on population and environment see also articles in the readers compiled by *Sprenger* (1991) or *Schenk-Sandbergen* (1991-1/2).

Besides the statements outlined above, it would be interesting if a compilation of detailed studies would be produced on the connection between population, poverty, appropriation of resources by foreign countries, from a gender perspective and linking macro-, meso- and microlevel. But, as it is stated in the NGO Treaty on Population and Environment formulated at the Global Forum 1992: such studies always have to be within the framework and boundaries set by ethics and human rights. The treaty itself outlines a basic ethics to deal with the issue *(Pollard et al.* 1992). Studies incorporating all these concerns would be very complex, but they would feed the environmental debates and policies with useful arguments.

It is worthwhile to compare the issues discussed above with ideas on population found back in policy documents (chapter 6, esp. 6.1)

4.4 Technology: reproductive technology and biotechnology

There has been a substantial debate on technology and its role in the development process. In a more scientific way, concepts at the basis of modern technology have been criticized (e.g. by feminist critics of science, mentioned in 3.3, see overview of discussions in *Braidotti et al.* 1993). Also, many case studies have been carried out which reveal the sometimes devastating effects of foreign technologies introduced in fragile social and ecosystems.[2] *Cynthia Bicocci et al.* (1990) have produced an annotated bibliography on secundary literature on women, gender and technology (in general) with publications of the last ten years. Substantial work analyzing the impact of technologies on gender and environment in combination, is scarce.

In this guide, I chose to discuss the subject with an example found in the literature, which may reflect on the link between the oppression of women and nature: reproductive technology and biotechnology. *Patricia Hynes* (1989-1 and 2) argues that the simultaneous oppression of women and nature (as described in 3.3) is still evident, by drawing the parallel between biotechnology in agriculture and reproductive technology. Biotechnology is "reducing nature to a pool of genetic units which can be spliced and recombined with the arrogant claim of improving on nature". Reproductive technology similarly is "reducing women to egg hatcheries and wombs for hire in order to manufacture life better than woman can birth". *Vandana Shiva* (1989), as discussed in chapter 2, elaborates further on these ideas, criticizing Western patriarchy and reductionist science for "maldevelopment", in which the marginalization of women and nature occurs simultaneously (see also 3.3). In a flaming speech (1991) she draws the same parallel as Hynes.[3] Patriarchy has constructed the male as active and the female (including nature) as passive. Creativity became the monopoly of men who were viewed as engaged in production, while women were viewed as engaged in mere reproduction (supposedly non-creative). Nature became only a "resource". She states: "Agricultural development under the patriarchal view sees cycles of fertility (either in nature or in the female body, hvdh) as limits that need to be broken, and views the breaking of limits as symbols of transcendence and power".

In both technologies, ownership of life is transmitted to the one who owns the technology. In biotechnology by splitting the organic bond between farmer and natural resources: farmers need to buy their seed from the companies that have the monopoly on its regeneration. In reproductive technology by splitting the organic bond between women and their children: women's reproduction is increasingly managed by medical experts. The argument for introducing something like patent rights is to "protect" the seed against "illegal" use by the farmer! In the case of reproduction, the parallel can be drawn with fetal rights, aiming to "protect" the foetus against its mother. In fact the development of both types of technology implies appropriation of life by technocrats in different forms.

Hynes mentions many astonishing facts about women's reproductive health. She states that what has changed since *Rachel Carson's* "Silent Spring" (1962, in which Carson pointed out the hazards of broad spectrum pesticides) until this time with its biotechnology, are mainly the metaphors. Pesticide companies openly declared war on nature in the '60s, biotechnologists are now claiming to "help nature" in preserving genetic diversity and in feeding the world population. Both biotechnology and reproductive technology, Hynes argues, are technological turnkeys for problems that are in fact social and political. Promotors of technology generally lack the expertise and the incentive to analyze the risks of the technologies for human health and the environment, while neither the social, political and spiritual prices are taken into consideration (*Hynes* (ed) 1989-1/2).[4]

Much more could be said about Northern commercial interests to control the natural heritage of species, on reproduction and women's rights etc, but it goes beyond the scope of this guide.

4.5 War and militarism

In the scarce literature on the subject I came across, war and militarism are regarded either as causes, but also as consequences of environmental degradation![5] *Marilyn Waring* (1988-1/2), elaborating on the exclusion of women and nature from macroeconomic calculation (see 4.1) concludes that national income estimates everywhere continue to be an assesment of how best to pay for the war. The whole of production and services as related to war and militarism adds to a high Gross National Product *(Schrijvers* 1993).[6] On the other hand, military expenditures, the arms trade and armed conflicts deprive billions of human beings of basic security and well being, reads the "Women's Action Agenda 21" *(World Women's Congress* 1992). Research, development and production of weapons, testing, maneuvers, and the presence of military bases, disposal of toxic materials, transport and resource use related to the military, all have a disastrous environmental impact. *Rosalie Bertell* (1991) and *Renate Walter* (1991) testify on military activities and (nuclear) pollution, stating that their burden is falling disproportionately on women and children, who lack the power to protest. *Magda Renner* (1991) testifies on refugees, (at least 75% women and children) who have fled because of war, preparation for war and environmental disruption caused by the industrialization process. "Wars have always been followed by harsh periods of poverty, famine, social/cultural/environmental disruption, but nothing is comparable to the devastating impact on all living beings caused by modern warfare".

The vicious circle
Olivia Bennett (1991) edited a book by 11 Sahelian writers, called "Greenwar". In the complex web of causes leading to social and political instability, bloodshed and war, environmental degradation is playing an increasingly important role. This is called the "greenwar factor". The writers' personal views and stories describe the complex vicious circle of "environmental impoverishment", increasing conflict over resources, marginalization of rural people, social and political unrest, displacement and uncontrolled migration, together leading to violence and armed conflict again adding to environmental degradation.

It is examined how traditional competition for resources can escalate into open conflict, and how the state can be a catalyst in this process. The state often supports certain types of agriculture, neglects certain areas and groups (rural population, esp. pastoralists and women), and fails to recognize and deal with environmental disaster. Sometimes it directly encourages violence and reacts with military violence to keep the unrest down. To this the authors add in their analysis global factors such as unequal terms of world trade and falling commodity prices, and the strangling influence of the debt crisis. "Aid in this context cannot have any profound or longlasting effect". Nafissa Abdel Rahim's contribution shows the situation of women environmental refugees in the Sudan.

Similarly, *Vandana Shiva* (1988-1 and 1991-2) elaborates on conflicts over natural resources in India.
Wendy Harcourt (1991-2), searches for a gender perspective of security. This security is not just about balancing numbers of armies and bombs, it also means food security, social security, human rights. Especially because conflict is mostly based on an imbalance between resources and people's needs, she claims the environment is another major security issue. Women as crisis managers bear the brunt of the unmanageable and insecure situations that follow from war, overexploitation and pollution. This brings us to the issue of food security.

4.6 Food security

A prominent gendered environmental issue is food security. In fact it reflects all the above mentioned issues. Furthermore, the issue shows the strong relations between macro, meso and microlevel processes. Food security is to be ensured at all levels (from individual to international), and yet jeopardized at all these different levels. Food security is endangered by deficient statistics, undervaluing or neglecting women's work and natural resources, because these statistics support policies that thwart women's work as food producers and environmental managers (see 4.1). Factors like debt and structural adjustment aggravate this situation (4.2). Related to this is the problem of resource appropriation for Northern consumerism (4.3), and national agricultural policies and technology all favouring export cropping above food production. Food security is also jeopardized by international and internal conflicts destroying the resource base and shutting down food distribution channels (4.5). Then, there is the population pressure on the remaining resources (4.3). Finally, food security is weakened at the local level by gender inequalities and sexual division of labour, where women have the main responsibility for the supply of food, fuelwood and water but lack the time and sufficient control over (depleting) resources to be able to do this in a sustainable way (next chapter). These mechanisms are outlined by *Philip Raikes* (1988-1/2), *Sen and Grown 1985/87*, *Lappé and Collins 1986/88, Bernstein et al. 1990 and Engo Tjeda 1991-1.*

Most writers refer to women's large share in food production. Dankelman and Davidson (1988) mention 80% for Sub Saharan Africa, 50-60% for Asia, 30% for Latin America. These percentages are increasing because of the increasing number of women-headed households caused by male outmigration (in which environmental degradation plays a role).

The destruction of ecologically sound indigenous technology (by "the development project"), often created and used by women, along with the destruction of their material base, is generally believed to be responsible for the feminization of poverty in societies that have had to bear the cost of environmental destruction, according to *Rosemary Brown* (1991).

By offering technical solutions to political and social problems, Europe and the United States have concentrated resources on wealthier farmers and more fertile areas, in the process often excluding the poor, writes *Philip Raikes* (1988-2). In Africa, seasonal and exceptional food shortage especially hits women who live alone, he argues, not only because they have smaller plots and more limited access to labour and credit, but because in many societies they are regarded as the food providers, not as the people to be provided for. In the Women's Action Agenda (World Women's Congress 1992) it is stated that, especially because the nutrition of the family is dependent on women's ability to produce food, and on the other hand women and children are the majority of the hungry, women's access to food, land tenure and ownership must be regarded as a basic human right.

In the issues discussed above, international and national factors are both influential. It would be relevant to outline certain examples of national strategies towards development, and their consequences for gender and the environment. Choices whether or not to focus on industrialization, urbanization, modernization of agriculture, can be weighed on their effects on the division of labour, the position of women and men, and the environment. As with the issue of debts and structural adjustment, literature analyzing the effects of national policies on gender and environment in combination is scarce. Also, in the scope of this guide it goes too far to elaborate on national examples.

A number of international, regional and national policy documents will be dealt with in chapter 5. Despite the need for solutions on higher levels, they tend to focus on the microlevel.

Of course this level is where the link between gender, environment and development is most evident. In chapter 5, I try to give a brief overview of two relevant issues at the local level which are closely linked to the issues outlined above.

Notes

1   It is in fact the reductionist way of looking at the forest as an economic resource which allows the unwise exploitation. Of course the forest is an economic resource, but the fact should be acknowledged that it is an ecosystem as well, and ecological principles have to be taken into account in its management. This is also a matter of control: if different actors (including local women and men) would be given a voice in the management the

monocrop approach would not survive, because diverse needs demand diverse production.

2   I refer to the library of LUW (Wageningen Agricultural University), the CML (Center for Environmental Studies Leiden), VENA documentation centre on women and autonomy (Leiden).

3   More thoroughly argued, and more convincing than *Hynes*, but being a speech, lacking references to literature.

4   Biotechnology and reproductive technology are also legal and human rights issues.

5   War and militarism may also be regarded as an issue reflecting the simultaneous oppression of women and nature, in which sexual violence is a common instrument. The literature dealt with does not discuss this issue.

6   *Ewa Charkiewicz* (1993) explains this briefly, based on *Waring* (1988). *Schrijvers* (1993) discusses the different forms of violence occurring in the world's economic development.

CHAPTER 5

Local issues: two representative examples

Much is written from the sectoral scope. The books of *Dankelman and Davidson* (1988) *Shiva* (1989) or *Rodda* (1991) or *Dankelman's* paper (1991-1) summarize women's activities in agriculture, forestry, energy and water supply, and the difficulties women face in performing these tasks because of environmental problems.

Agriculture, forestry, energy and water supply are intimately connected, both in an ecological sense and through women's work. Therefore a cross-sectoral approach to GED is a prerequisite to deal with environmental problems and women's position sufficiently. Furthermore, in the scope of this guide,it would not be possible to go into all the different "sectors". For these two reasons I chose two relevant cross-sectoral issues; women's health as an explicitly gendered environmental problem, and natural resource management from a gender point of view. The chosen issues represent two sides of the spectrum of women's roles in environmental matters. The first theme ultimately reflects the victimization of women by environmental degradation and pollution, although it must be stressed that in keeping the family healthy they are key actors themselves. The second theme focuses on the knowledge and skills of women as environmental managers, their possibilities and constraints as results of gender, and other cultural, political and economic factors.

5.1 Environmental problems and women's health

Women, as suppliers of clean water, food and shelter, and often knowledgeable about medicinal plants and caring, play an essential role in keeping the family healthy *(Dankelman* 1991-1). The literature on GED, however, reveals that for women "bearing the brunt" of environmental degradation, either by heavier workloads, inferior nutrition or direct pollution, finally means a deteriorating health for themselves and their children. A publication on women and forest resources by *FAO/SIDA* (1989) and an article on energy by *Elisabeth*

Cecelski (1987-2) describe the spiral of environmental and health deterioration. For example, through environmental degradation women have less woodfuel, and less time for cooking and for food supply, which forces them to cut back on the number of cooked meals and their nutritional value. Carrying the heavy headloads of fuel over long distances causes exhaustion and pains. Often crop residues or animal dung (both possible fertilizers) have to be used instead of woodfuel, with a detrimental effect on soil fertility, and thus the food cultivation. Furthermore, cooking is the most serious occupational health hazard, because of the smoke from open fires, aggravated by the use of inferior fuel materials. So, the lack of good woodfuel has a number of negative consequences for (women's) health.

Because of their tasks as water suppliers, women are more subject to water-related diseases. The International Drinking Water Supply and Sanitation Decade supposedly has meant a giant step forward in this respect *(Smyke* 1991, van *Wijk-Sijbesma* 1985, *INSTRAW* 1989).

Patricia Smyke (1991) in her book on women and health, puts that environmental health hazards depend on the kind of work, and the amount of work. Of course the environment itself is important: in the urban environment air pollution, heat, noise, toxic chemicals and radiation are special problems (see: reader *Schenk-Sandbergen* 1991-1/2). *Hardoy et al.* (1990) in their book on housing and health in Third World cities, make special reference to women. In their first chapter: "in many low income settlements there may be a significantly higher incidence of certain diseases among women, spending more time within the settlement and its contaminated environment". For example women suffer more from inadequate water supplies and sanitation, and show more respiratory problems associated with smokey living environments. *Mirjam Letsch* (1993) describes the influence of class (esp. extreme poverty), caste and gender on participation in a specific water and sanitation project in the urban context. In general, there is a scarcity of literature on gender and health in the urban context.

Poisoning and pollution
A serious threat for women (and unborn children) comes from the use of pesticides that are often forbidden in the North, and dumped in Southern countries. These pesticides may be especially harmful to women because of their high illiteracy rate or the inability to read the language on the label. However even more important is women's lack of power to protest against the use of these pesticides and their own bad

working conditions. Among the consequences there are miscarriages and stillbirths. (See *Chee Yoke Ling* on Malaysia, e.g. 1989, and the work of *Rachel Carson* 1962).

Rosalie Bertell (1991) testifies on nuclear pollution and its radiation primarily in Northern and Eastern European countries, of which women are the worst victims. Some other testimonies from the *World Women's Congress* (1992) also elaborate on the issue of pollution. As women form the majority of the poor hungry and illiterate people on earth, *Lezak Shallat* (1990) argues, they are the most vulnerable to all health hazards and calamities, not just those posed by a sick environment. Moreover, women themselves have become a "hazardous environment" for the unborn, with wombs "more sump than sanctuary" (according to Lin Nelson in *Diamond and Orenstein* 1990). *Shallat* mentions many examples of poisoning, pollution and reproductive health in her article, as do *Martin-Brown and El-Hinnawi* (1988).

In an Australian document on sustainable development it is argued that it is likely that poor people (70% of whom are women in Australia) in Northern countries run also higher environmental risks by being over-represented in urban fringes and industrial areas *(Brown and Switzer* 1991). They disproportionaly bear the burden of hazards such as landfills, polluting factories and toxic waste dumps *(Shallat* 1990, e.g. *Barten* 1992). Many examples of health effects of environmental degradation in Southern countries, as well as women's initiatives to ameliorate the situation occur in *Dankelman and Davidson* (1988), for the rural as well as the urban context.

Marginalization and powerlessness
In a very useful paper about the effects of environmental factors on women's health, *Jacqueline Sims* (Sims/WHO 1990) puts it clearly: "The root cause of environmentally derived health hazards to women is not so much the environmental factors themselves, but rather the social forces which determine women's exposure to such hazards, coupled with the vulnerability of their biological function as reproducers. These forces can be summarized in two words – marginalization and (resulting) powerlessness. The greatest symptom of marginalization and powerlessness is lack of time for their tasks and leisure to maintain their health. Women's drudgery, at the same time forms an effective mode for social control". She refers to *Anoja Wickramasinghe* (1989) who shows for Sri Lanka that women achieve their multiple roles only at the

expense of leisure and sleep, not assisted by men because of the stringent sexual division of labour. *Anil Agarwal* outlines (1985-2) how some cultural traditions in India make hygiene difficult for women, and thus have negative effects on their health.

Together, all these publications reveal the fact that worldwide, impoverishment, power relations (gendered among them) and the subjection to environmental degradation and pollution are closely tied.

5.2 Natural resources management

Ruvimbo Chimedza (1989) states that ideas about natural resources management are often restricted to wildlife ranging, afforestation and soil conservation as a national target within an institutional setting. Farmers, however, are closely involved in the management of the basic natural resources. African women, providing 80% of subsistence food, are involved in this management with the primary aim of ensuring household food security.

According to *Stone and Molnar* (1986-1) there is a paucity of literature directly addressing women's tasks and responsibilities in natural resource management and environmental degradation. This is supposedly due to the fact that women appear to have less responsibility in management, because the control of natural resources is mostly in the hands of men (this crucial issue is dealt with further on). Yet women's distinct work and family functions and the unique obstacles they face in gaining access to resources, services and training have significant consequences for their management of natural resources and make them an important subject for study. Stone and Molnar compiled a bibliography on labor inputs and time allocation, women's role in agriculture, access to credit and inputs, marketing and price policies, extension and training, education, watersupply management and sanitation, all before 1986(Stone 1986-2). Since then much more literature on the tasks and the role of women, especially in issues like forestry and agriculture has appeared (see index).

Gender and women's roles
Often the issue of women and natural resources is studied in the context of development projects, and detailed descriptions of indigenous management are scarce.[1] The sexual division of labour makes that women and men acquire different domains of knowledge and skills with respect to natural resources management. *Irene Dankelman* (1991-1)

argues that through their occupation with food collection, women developed knowledge on plant breeding, which was a requirement for agriculture to settle. Probably rice, sorghum and other grains have been domesticated by women, and techniques like hoeing, using the spade, mulching and terracing are probably inventions of women. They mainly manage the biomass flows from one "sector" (or part of the farming system) to another: fodder from the forest to the animals, natural fertilizers from the forest to the fields, manure from animals to the fields, crop production to animals, etc. These processes are essential for the sustainability of agro-ecosystems *(Dankelman and Shiva* 1991-2). *Dankelman and Davidson* (1988) highlight the roles of women in the management of land, water and forestry. As food and cashcrop producers, women act as landmanagers e.g. by flexible cropping patterns, and seed selection. Women are responsible for water collecting, storing, purifying etc. With respect to forestry women are often involved in agroforestry development[2], in establishing tree nurseries etcetera. But in their book they focus mostly on how these tasks are thwarted by environmental degradation and how women have organized themselves, more than on the nature of their strategies to cope with the resources (as is the case in *ELC/Forum* '85, 1986).

Although there is little disagreement about the importance of women in managing natural resources, *Colette Dehlot* in a contribution to *Rodda* (1991) states that the knowledge about the link of women and natural resources remains scant. There is a lack of literature on individual and institutional roles in environmental degradation and conservation. In many instances, women especially in Africa have employed trial and error systems involving intercropping, multicropping, agroforestry, soil regeneration etc. Also they contribute to the conservation of biodiversity of the natural environment, which is largely unrecognized. But the above-mentioned activities, and for example fish processing, fuelwood collection, anti-desertification measures (in the Sahel), are all thwarted by large scale exploitation, population density and misconceptions about the value of traditional activities on the part of development agencies. Traditional natural resource management often implies culturally-bound environmental protection, in which gender may play an important role (for example, only women may use a certain tree, so that the resource is not over exploited, tasks are clearly defined etc.). *Dianne Rocheleau* has written interesting articles and papers on gender and agroforestry (e.g. 1985-2, 1987, 1991). Note also her "multiple user approach" par 7.2.

Pools of knowledge

Grass-roots organizations can be a pool of knowledge on natural resources management. These organizations are often suitable to be strengthened in their efforts to work towards sustainable management and conservation. They have often developed answers to environmental degradation like the selection of drought resistant species, mulching, energy saving, and waste recycling *(Dehlot* 1991). In this respect the research findings of *WEDNET* (Women Environment and Development Network), coordinated by ELCI, may be interesting. They seek to document and legitimize African women's indigenous knowledge on natural resource management. Research findings are to be expected; proceedings of the research projects can be found in their magazine *WEDNEWS. Rosemary Jommo,* WEDNET coordinator, in a speech: "As one listens to the women recount their perceptions of resource use and underlying linkages, one gets glimpses of economy and resource management based on a sophisticated web of kinship ties and communal access and control". WEDNET found some factors which affect women's management: declining capacity of communities to secure agricultural production, drought and declining access to water, commoditization of land, privatization of common property, outmigration of male labour and cultural and socio-economic structures. In researching grass-roots practices concerning natural resources management, there is the pitfall of the appropriation of knowledge by outsiders, which does not serve the empowerment of the knowledgeable women *(Jommo* 1992).

Legal aspects of environmental management

Sometimes women are too easily called "environmental managers", because of their tasks in the supply of fuel, fodder, water etc. There is a difference between use and management, management implies that deliberate measures are taken to increase or sustain the resource and its yield. In fact, real management is only possible when the manager has control over the resources, and poor women often lack this (often one should rather speak of women as "potential managers"). Therefore a crucial issue for natural resources management is women's access and especially control over land, water and forest resources. Interesting in this respect is a workshop document from *ILO* (1988) sketching the African and Asian situation of women's access to land. In Africa, women's access has been marginalized by colonialism in the past, and by structural adjustment and population growth in the present. For women to fulfill their tasks, ensuring access is not enough. They must also be able to control land resources, have production inputs secured, and control the disposal of the output. Control is essential in the future sustainability of small-holder food production. In Asia, in a situation of landlessness, socialist and collective ownership, resettlement and/or landreform, women are the most vulnerable, because they are the poorest and disadvantaged competitors for wage labour and entitlement. Also, access to common and forest lands becomes more and more restricted. *Elisabeth Cecelski* (1987-1/2) and *Dianne Rocheleau* (1985-2, and in *Raintree* 1987) address women's tenure as related to energy and agroforestry respectively. *Prah* (1991) elaborates on sex and access in the livestock, fisheries and wildlife sectors in Eastern and Southern Africa. Also useful in this respect is the reader compiled by *Edith van Walsum* (1989), including some case-studies on access and control issues, and ownership and management of livestock.

Gender and the wider context
The literature on the subject generally uses scattered examples as proof that women are the best environmental managers. Men's roles are rarely made explicit. There is not much literature yet on *gender* and natural resources management, investigating the differences and relations between men's and women's practices, possibilities and constraints. There may be many examples of gendered practices as found in ecologically sustainable traditional farming systems, but as far as I know there is not yet a comprehensive, informative book with case-studies on natural resources management and gender. In the magazine *Gender Studies in Agriculture*, compiled by Joke Webbink, many abstracts of case-studies can be found. *Poats et al.* (1988) present many case-studies of gender in farming systems from all over the world.[3]

There is a special need for literature which links these gendered local practices to a wider setting. As *Caren Levy* (1992) puts it: conceptualizing the gender-environment link only on the local level as men's and women's use of natural resources, easily results in blaming the individual. The activities are part of a wider system of production and consumption which are supported and maintained by economic and political interests (in which gender ideologies play a role as well).

This implies the need to change national and international policy in favour of women's management capacity and possibilities. The next chapter outlines how the linkage between gender (mainly women) and natural resources has been recognized in policy documents.

Notes

1 The (218!) casestudies of the *Global Assembly* (1991) are not detailed on the natural resources management practices, but only briefly outline how women have organized to counteract environmental degradation.

2 Agroforestry is the deliberate cultivation of annual crops and perennial crops (trees, shrubs) on the same piece of land. Because of their diverse tasks, agroforestry is often a good option for women. See e.g. *Rocheleau* (1985-2, 1987).

3 IIED in London is developing an audiovisual training set on gender and natural resources management, which will probable be ready by the autumn of 1993.

CHAPTER 6

GED in policy documents

This chapter deals with GED in policy documents; specifically with respect to the gradual recognition of the importance of the theme and policy alternatives. I will review some international, multilateral, Dutch and some Southern policy writings. It is mostly policy rhetoric, and policy recommendations that one comes accross. Often the question: "how?" will emerge, because vagueness is a major feature. However, I feel it is useful to investigate the trend in thinking on GED within an influential funding organization like the World Bank, international programmes like UNEP, or the UNCED process, all having a worldwide impact. The second paragraph elaborates on Dutch policy, where the connection between the elements of GED has only recently been made. Finally two documents on GED are presented, that may serve as examples for the formulation of a regional and a national plan for gender aware sustainable development. Hopefully the results of (more of) these policies will be critically reviewed and documented in the near future.

6.1 International policy

In the introduction, I sketched the recently established link between environmental and gender concern in international policy. *Dankelman and Davidson* (1988) have outlined the response to the issue of women and environment by different international organizations, such as IUCN and a number of bilateral and multilateral donor agencies up to 1988.

Conservation and sustainable development
In 1980, *IUCN/UNEP/WWF* launched the World Conservation Strategy, which was enriched with gender considerations during a conference in 1987, *(IUCN* 1987-1-2/see also 1988, *Soepardjo Roestam* 1987). In 1990 the General Assembly of IUCN adopted two relevant resolutions on gender issues (full texts given by *van den Oever* 1991).

The first World Conservation Strategy did not even incorporate social and economic concerns, but these are addressed in the second

Strategy *(Mitlin* 1992). This second Strategy, launched in 1991, includes a section on recognizing and extending the role of women in the community. The gender issue appears every now and then throughout the text. Women appear in relation to literacy: bringing female and male literacy to the same level is set as a target. Women are also mentioned in relation to the "population issue": e.g. it is stated that their status should be improved in order for them to have less children. Participatory research would be recommendable, to take proper account of the roles of men and women. Furthermore, it is stated, women must be able to participate in decision-making with regard to common resources and contribute their expertise as environmental managers *(IUCN et al.* 1991).

In 1987 the report of the "Brundtland commission" ("Our Common Future", *WCED* 1987), links environment and development into its concept of sustainable development, dealing with population, food security, loss of biodiversity, energy, industry, human settlements. It mentions women's crucial roles in "population and human resources", and "food security", but conclusions and recommendations concerning women and sustainable development are lacking *(Dankelman* 1987).[1]

UNEP

A catalyzing role in the international recognition of women and environment as an issue, has been played by the United Nations Environmental Programme (UNEP), which was created on the recommendation of the Stockholm Conference in 1972. UNEP was the brain behind the resolutions on the environment as found in the Nairobi Forward Looking Strategies for the Advancement of Women *(UN* 1986).[2]

UNEP also initiated the women and environment workshop in the NGO parallel conference at the time. The report of this workshop, organized by the organization ELC[3] *(ELC/Forum* '85 1986) contains the conference results and a resolution in which women and the environment are mentioned. It urges "Women to be more conscious of the crucial role they play in environmental and natural resource management", and asks UNEP in turn to provide information on "how women can play an active role in combatting serious environmental problems". In UNEP's own "State of the Environment" the role of women is highlighted (*UNEP* 1988 and 1992).

UNCED

Appointed by the UN as the leading agency on women and environment

78

in the UN system, UNEP installed a Senior Women's Advisory Group
that organized the Regional Assemblies and the Global Assembly on
Women and the Environment (see *Loudiyi et al.* 1988, *Ofosu-Amaah*
1991, and *Global Assembly* 1991 and 1992), used in the preparatory
process towards the United Nations Conference on Environment and
Development *(UNCED)*.

In the official UNCED process, the Resolution on Women,
Environment and Development, in which women are called "active and
equal participants" in ecosystem management, was agreed upon
internationally *(UNCED/Prepcom III* 1991-1, preparations see *Alders/ UNCED*
1991). An overview of women and environment in the UNCED process
until Prepcom III is given by *UNCED/Filomina Chioma Steady* (1991-1)
and *Caroline de Jong-Boon/ FEMCONSULT* (1992).[4]

In the final Declaration of Rio de Janeiro, one of the 27 Principles is:
"Women have a vital role in environmental management and
development. Their full participation is therefore essential to achieve
sustainable development" (*UNCED* 1992-1).

In "Agenda 21" a special chapter is dedicated to women, one of the
"major groups" whose role should be strengthened (*UNCED* 1992-2). The
basis for action with regard to women are the Nairobi Forward Looking
Strategies for Women *(UN* 1986), and several earlier conventions against
gender-based discrimination. The implementation of these programmes
is considered critical to the implementation of the Agenda. In this chapter
priorities for research and action are outlined. I consider it relevant to
mention all the objectives proposed for national governments which are,
next to the implementation of the Forward Looking Strategies:

- to increase the proportion of women decision-makers, planners,
  technical advisers, managers and extension workers in environment
  and development fields;
- to consider developing and issuing by the year 2000 a strategy of
  changes necessary to eliminate constitutional, legal, administrative,
  cultural, behavioural, social and economic obstacles to women's full
  participation in sustainable development and in public life;
- to establish by the year 1995 mechanisms at the national, regional and
  international levels to assess the implementation and impact of
  development and environment policies and programmes on women
  and to ensure their contributions and benefits;
- to assess, review, revise and implement, where appropriate, curricula
  and other educational material, with a view to promoting the
  dissemination to both men and women of gender-relevant knowledge

and valuation of women's roles through formal and non-formal education, as well as through training institutions, in collaboration with non-governmental organizations;
- to formulate and implement clear governmental policies and national guidelines, strategies and plans for the achievement of equality in all aspects of society, including the promotion of women's literacy, education, training, nutrition and health and their participation in key decision-making positions and in management of the environment, particularly as it pertains to their access to resources, by facilitating better access to all forms of credit, particularly in the informal sector, taking measures towards ensuring women's access to property rights as well as agricultural inputs and implements;
- to implement, as a matter of urgency, in accordance with country-specific conditions, measures to ensure that women and men have the same right to decide freely and responsibly the number and spacing of their children and have access to information, education and means, as appropriate, to enable them to exercize this right in keeping with their freedom, dignity and personally held values;
- to consider adopting, strengthening and enforcing legislation prohibiting violence against women and to take all necessary administrative, social and educational measures to eliminate violence against women in all its forms.

Among the proposed activities to reach these objectives are:
- to implement measures to strengthen and empower women's bureaus, NGOs and groups in capacity building;
- to implement measures to eliminate illiteracy and increase access to education for girls and women;
- to promote the reduction of the heavy workload of women and girls by nurseries and kindergartens, the equal sharing of household tasks between men and women and environmentally sound technologies;
- to implement "Programmes to establish and strengthen preventive and curative health facilities, which include women-centred, women-managed, safe and effective reproductive health care and affordable, accessible, responsible planning of family size and services, as appropriate, in keeping with freedom, dignity and personally held values".

It is also proposed to develop consumer awareness, emphasizing women's crucial role in achieving changes necessary to reduce or eliminate unsustainable patterns of consumption and production.

Urgent action is required to avert the ongoing "environmental and economic degradation", and to ensure women's involvement in decision-making and implementation of activities. Some recommendations for research, data collection and dissemination of information are given.

Although sometimes vague, and difficult for governments to implement, the outlined objectives and activities seem to be a reasonable basis for further action.

UNIFEM (1992) has listed all specific recommendations on women throughout "Agenda 21" in a booklet. Women are referred to in most chapters. In the rhetoric the necessity of women's participation and empowerment are acknowledged. The booklet may serve policy makers, NGOs and researchers in justifying their work on the issue of gender and environment. However, it is as important to analyze the UNCED documents integrally on their gender aspects. The Women's Environment and Development Organization will come with an analysis in the near future (WEDO, forthcoming).

Reviewing the rhetoric: the World Bank
Recently in the international development community the rhetoric has come to recognize the links of GED. Still, the nuances in formulation differ and seem to lay bare the ideas about gender and development behind the policies. Often women are viewed (or have to be presented as such to the donors!) as instruments to ameliorate the environment, or even to guarantee environmental "project success". Here follow two examples of policy recommendations presented to the World Bank, which seem to reveal that environmental concerns are valued over gender concerns.

Susan Joekes (1989) in a paper for the Bank argues that women's programmes contribute to sustainable development for three reasons:
1 The improvement of women's economic position relieves some of their pressure on common property resources.
2 Their improved position modifies the incentive for bearing children.
3 Environmental programmes and women's programmes share a common goal of asset creation. For example: increasing women's (groups) ownership rights over natural resources serves both their independence and better environmental management.

Julia Clones, in a report on women's crucial role in managing the environment in Sub-Saharan Africa (SSA, *Clones/World Bank* 1991): "there is a clear convergence between environmentally sound and sustainable development and the improved status of women in SSA". She mentions interventions required to address women's legal, economic and political status, in order to ensure that they are actively and effectively involved in environmental conservation for sustainable development. These are:

1   Increasing gender sensitivity at the policy making level by training.
2   Gender responsive policy formulation. Ensure women's participation in all levels of decision-making. Address their short term needs and "structural integration in the long term development process".
3   Provision of financial, technical, educational and information tools.
4   Participation. "There is a general concensus among development experts and donors that popular participation would result in improved design and implementation of development projects".

In addition to these, more or less instrumental interventions, Clones mentions also:

5   Empowerment of women. Projects should add to women's access to and control over natural resources and the socioeconomic system.

Clones (1991) also outlines the World Bank's policy regarding environmental concerns. Not until 1989 did the World Bank make an "environmental assesment operational directive" for the projects which they finance. The Bank's recent initiatives on environment and development, are the Global Environment Facility (funding, in cooperation with UNEP and UNDP), and the National Environmental Action Plans. The Action Plans have been in operation since 1987 (as a response to the weak implementation of the World Conservation Strategy), but the gender connection was not made until a workshop in 1990 which concluded that "Women and Environment should be an issue". The policy of the Bank has not gone much further than that.[5]

By donor agencies, some governments and on an international level, women's issues and environmental factors are addressed, but it seems more difficult to link the issues in the implementation of their policies. *Caren Levy* reaffirms this, stating that although in international policy, research and activism the link between gender and environmental concerns is becoming stronger, governmental bureaucracies mostly fail to link the issues sufficiently. Both gender and environment are cross-cutting issues, suitable to break with the scale based and sectoral approaches in the development assistance tradition. Unfortunately so far the issues have never been sufficiently linked in development assistance (*Levy* 1992). The Dutch situation may serve as an example.

6.2 Dutch policy

In 1986 the commission on Ecology and Development Cooperation recognized women's special relationship with the environment and their key role in the management of natural resources. They stated that women's direct involvement in environmentally sound development should be advanced as special area of attention (*Commissie Ecologie* 1986).

The Dutch parliamentary policy document on international cooperation "A World of Difference" states that especially women are victimized by the (international) market penetrating into their communities and the break-down of traditional management systems. Women also possess the knowledge about natural resources, and for these reasons it is evident that women should again be visible in rural development policy, that their role should be strengthened, in the interest of themselves and in the interest of the society (*Tweede Kamer* 1990). The report clings to economic growth as the core of development, a concept which the National Environmental Policy Plan (*VROM* 1990) leaves behind.

In the Netherlands' National Report to UNCED (*VROM* 1991), it is stated that the ultimate aim of Dutch national and international policy will be sustainable development as defined by the Brundtland Commission (*WCED* 1987). Through multilateral and bilateral cooperation the Dutch government seeks to enforce the implementation of environmental policy. It mentions women (whose "role and position should be strengthened") only in the context of population policy, which is introduced as an environmental issue without explanation. A remark is added on the resources wasted on animal husbandry in the Netherlands, unfortunately without further comments on the connection of the issue of population and overconsumption in that section.[6] Support is declared for low external input agriculture and natural resource management, land reform programmes and projects, and energy. The focus is on the transfer of know-how to and awareness-raising in developing countries.

Two spearheads of development policy
"Women and Development", and "Environment and Development" are two seperate programs of the Dutch Ministry of International Cooperation, and both spearheads of their policy (together with poverty alleviation in urban areas, and research).

The spearhead Women and Development expresses in a series of papers *(Ministry* 1989-1990) that "while the improvement of position and status of women is fully valid as an emancipatory end in itself, the utilization of women's potential is at the same time an efficient means to improve the quality of development as a whole". In 1987 the Women and Development Action Programme *(Ministry* 1987) appeared, the first comprehensive statement on Women and Development, in a "more operational direction". It lists a number of strongly interdependent objectives, among which:

- to improve women's access to and control over production factors (et al.);
- to increase women's involvement in decision-making, improve the organization of women at all levels, and
- to encourage exchange of information and communication between women and women's groups (et al.).

However, they state in the series of papers, "these objectives fall largely outside the scope of the series, which must focus on first arrangements for the actual and beneficial involvement of women in familiar project settings". Again it seems to be "dealing with practical problems first" without recognizing the strategic potential of interventions (see also 3.1).

Their sector paper "Women, energy, forestry and environment" *(Ministry* 1990) focuses in its succinct local level analysis on gender and its implications for women, among others concluding that the worst effects of degradation are passed to women, while the benefits of commercialization mainly end up with men. Lack of women's time keeps the vicious circle of poverty and degradation going on. They state: "the answer must somehow lie in rehabilitation of the environment, with women's time sufficiently freed, their scope of action sufficiently enlarged, and their shortterm and longterm benefits sufficiently ensured". This paper could be called a GED manual, and thus it will reappear in paragraph 7.2.

The Dutch government has developed an entrance test for development projects requesting funds. It aims to be an integrated impact assesment, doing justice to three spearheads of development: women, poverty and environment. The way this test is constructed shows that it is still very difficult to operationalize an integrated vision through the existing bureaucratic channels *(Ministry* 1992).

In its environmental document a Dutch NGO *(HIVOS* 1989, in Dutch) goes beyond the local level analysis of both environmental problems and solutions. Its policy is to strengthen local initiatives to reach higher, political goals. However, the document failed to emphasize on women's groups. Women are mentioned only as victims of degradation, and the recommendation is made that the organization's own "women's working group" and the "environmental working group" should coordinate their activities. Especially because the women's group should be aware of the danger that women's needs will be negatively affected by the overall attention paid to the environment This may be illustrative of the Dutch idea that the interests of women and the environment are opposed, which has to do with the fact that movements and institutions concerned with women's issues or environmental issues have hardly connected until now. The danger of conflicting interest is indeed real, when no integral policy is made.[7]

6.3 Some other examples

The next two documents may serve as examples for the formulation of a regional and a national plan for sustainable development respectively.

The African Women's Assembly *(Loudiyi et al.* 1988) proposes to involve women in the implementation of the Cairo Plan of Action, a plan made in 1986 by African Environmental Ministers at the initiative of UNEP. This Plan of Action aims to reverse environmental degradation and achieve energy and food self-sufficiency at the village level. The report gives recommendations on the regional, national and local scale, concerning environmental rehabilitation and women's participation, differentiated for four ecological zones.

A discussion paper for the Australian government identifies five interrelated policy principles for sustainable development at the national level:

1 protection of social equity,
2 safeguarding national and personal security. This is environmental protection from pollution, degradation, poverty and biological risks,
3 precautionary resource management (e.g. no increased economic risk for households),
4 full valuing of resources (including not only natural resources but also health, education and unpaid work), and
5 environmental education which includes women's concerns. For this principle it is considered important to have women representatives in environmental science and economics. This, because in the past, by their absence, many questions on ecologically sustainable

development from the fields of health, welfare, household management and social policy have neither been investigated nor included in environmental education *(Valerie Brown and Margaret Switzer* 1991).[8]
The paper contains many strategy recommendations for each policy principle, and may be a good example for other countries to follow. It may also be interesting to examine other National Reports that have been prepared for UNCED on their recognition of the GED connection.

Notes

1   Other critics of the Brundtlandt report are for example Berit As in *Linggard and Moberg* (1990), just like Dankelman discussing its neglect of women (see 2.2). *Thijs de la Court* (among many others) criticizes the report for its strong belief in economic growth and its western centred views (1990, 1991) Other critics of the report are to be found in the reader compiled by *Frijns/Hazeu* (1991), among them Ted Trainer.

2   *Hilkka Pietila and Jeanne Vickers* (1990) describe the history of UN policy on women in general.

3   Nowadays ELCI; Environment Liaison Centre International, a global membership organization for environmental NGOS, based in Nairobi. They played a role in organizing NGOS around UNCED as well (see *ELCI* 1992-1/2).

4   For more on international policy see 6.1. The women's preparatory meetings for UNCED are dealt with also in 2.2)

5   We've seen the criticism of World Banks's "environmental" policy from Susan George in paragraph 4.2. *HIVOS* in a policy paper (1989) also mentions the discrepancy between its rhetoric and practice on the environment. Different articles in the reader *Frijns/Hazeu* (1991) give the same picture.

6   The report mentions the inequitable distribution of resources worldwide as an issue in another context. For a discussion on the issue of overconsumption and population see 4.3.

7   *Boetes* (1990) summarizes the comments of the Dutch Emancipation Council on the National Environmental Policy Plan. Also here, the conflicting rather than the complementary interests are emphasised *(Emancipatieraad* 1990, see also *Gilden et al* 1990).

8   They use ecological terms about women and men who supposedly represent different "habitats" (range of the species' interactions with its physical environment) and have a differential use of the same environmental "niche" (role of the species in relation to resource flows).

CHAPTER 7

GED methodology: some tools and guidelines

Various methodological issues have emerged in previous chapters. In chapter 3 the political economy *(Adams* 1990) and the "political ecology" approach *(Blaikie and Brookfield* 1987) were discussed as approaches to assess sustainable development (3.2). The feminist critics of science have developed their own research methods. The ideas of gender planning *(Moser* 1986, 1989), and the autonomy concept *(Schrijvers* 1985, 1991), have been discussed in 3.1 and serve as a planning and analytical tool respectively. In chapter 4 some economists with alternative approaches to national income accounting were introduced, proposing more environment and gender sensitive accounting. Such alternative figures will be of great importance for development initiatives, but they are still in an initial phase. At the local level, the analysis of gender and environment also has its problems, as discussed in chapter 5.

This chapter focuses on applied, i.e. policy and project oriented research, meant for those trying to deal with gender and environment concerns within existing development channels. The first paragraph deals with specific gender analysis and planning, which may be useful when enriched with environmental concerns. The second paragraph examines some specific manuals and conceptual frameworks on gender and environment in combination. It must be stressed once again that a real "GED methodology" implies a change of policy and methodology, in all spheres and at all levels, and not only within existing development channels.

7.1 Gender analysis and planning

Although in the late '70s women's productive roles got more emphasis in Women and Development, there were not enough experts trained in the analysis of complex and variable matters such as the division of labour, decision-making and income management in households. The gender of the researcher is no guarantee that gender concerns are taken

sufficiently into account. Therefore, in the '80s, the need for a framework for gender analysis was recognized *(Poats et al.* 1988). A book that is widely used in training for this purpose is "Gender roles in development projects" by *Catherine Overholt et al.* (1985). It is a handbook providing a framework and set of basic concepts to be used in casestudy analysis, and seven case-studies are discussed at length. It emphasizes the link between development goals and gender differences in the "client population". The framework for project analysis entails the following research activities:
– an activity profile,
– an access and control profile,
– an analysis of factors influencing activities, access and control, and
– a project cycle analysis.
This is called the Harvard Analytical Framework.[1]

Susan Poats et al. (1988, 1989) show that gender proves to be the most useful category to disaggregate the farm household and analyze the dynamics within the household. Intra-household dynamics reflect gender-related responsibilities, access and control over resources, different income flows etc. Also, there are great differences between households caused by factors such as class, income, ethnicity, culture, and demographic variables. Therefore, neither between households, nor within households there is the assumed "trickle accross" of development benefits. Farming Systems Research and Extension (FSR/E) would be suitable to match with gender, because for instance women play a central role in the small low-income farming systems on which FSR/E focuses. Furthermore its "holistic, dynamic systems approach" would allow for a focus on the division of labour and an integration of farm and non-farm labour. Although the systems approach of FSR/E is not necessarily as "holistic and dynamic"[2] as the authors claim it to be, they present interesting examples of gender methodology in their impressive compilation of case-studies.[3]

Caroline Moser, in the publication discussed in 3.1, (i.e. *Moser* 1989-1) argues that gender planning lags behind because of the gender blindness of authorities, the lack of methodological tools, and the difficulties in integrating gender into the existing planning disciplines. She states that: "Women will always be marginalized in planning theory and practice until theoretical feminist concerns are adequately incorporated into a gender planning framework". Precizely because there is so much confusion about underlying assumptions of Women in Development, she identifies some simplified methodological tools. These tools can assist planners in the appraisal and evaluation of complex planning interventions, and the formulation of more gender aware proposals at policy, programme or project level within particular socioeconomic and political contexts.

From Canada comes a useful manual for Gender and Development: "Two halves make a whole" *(CCIC et al.* 1991). The gender analysis in this manual goes beyond the local level, combining elements of the Harvard Analytical Framework ("a useful data gathering tool but providing no guidance in determining development directions") with such concepts as women's subordination, strategic gender interests and the transformation of gender relations. Also inspired by *Moser,* the authors elaborate on conceptual tools for analysis. These are:
– the gender division of labour,
– types of labour,
– differential access and control of resources and benefits, and
– influencing factors (like the environment).
They also work out conceptual tools for defining development work. These are:
– women's condition (material) and position (social and economic status),
– practical needs and strategic interests,
– levels of participation (participants/ beneficiairies or agents) and
– the transformative potential of the programme or project.
Furthermore, they give guidelines for training on the subject *(CCIC et al.* 1991). It would be a challenge to better work out the natural resources aspects, especially within this framework.

7.2 GED manuals and frameworks for research

Some specific GED manuals and frameworks have seen the light of day. *J. Martin Brown and E. El-Hinnawi* (1988) have prepared a document on women and environment, based on experiences from various development organizations, containing many recommendations applicable for policy and projects from the local to the international level. They propose to offer women alternative livelihood options in degraded rural areas, and assess the environmental impact on women's health. They also propose all kinds of measures to assist women by means of legislation, organization, and education.

A gender manual for issues in agriculture and natural resource management has been written for USAID *(Russo et al.* 1989). Inspired by *Poats et al.* (1988) the manual explores how gender analysis can be used as a tool for better understanding the relationship between social, economic and technical factors at work in the agricultural and natural resources sector. Their (working) definition of gender: "a socioeconomic variable to analyze roles, responsibilities, constraints and opportunities of the people involved in the development effort. It considers both men and women and should not be confused as being an equity issue". They state that gender goes beyond the equity issue, and that it is an economic issue as well. In doing so, they neglect the crucial power dimension of gender. Their approach is terribly instrumental, women are dealt with as a human resource for project success. The authors may have done this for strategic purposes (see also World Bank papers 6.1), but an approach like this can never be in women's interest. They state for example that attention to gender issues can result in: elimination of bottlenecks to production, successful transfer of technology and willingness to adopt new practices!

A better example is the Dutch Women and Development sector paper on Energy, Forestry and Environment *(Ministry* 1990, discussed also in 6.2), which provides a checklist with questions on the following subjects:
1 The general picture and women's use of trees (questions related to intake, impact/design, women, trees and environment, and women's workload and time allocation).
2 The energy crisis and forestry.
3 Women's access to resources, and opportunities.
As discussed in 6.2, higher policy goals on women's empowerment are perceived as "largely outside the scope" of such manuals as these, focusing on familiar project settings. *Caren Levy* (1992) criticizes the checklist approach in general, her arguments are discussed below. Recently the Dutch ministry has prepared an integrated impact assesment for development projects (poverty/women/environment): *Ministry* (1992) (see also 6.2).

The Commonwealth Secretariat has provided an extensive manual for trainers in Africa on "Women, Conservation and Agriculture" *(Commonwealth Secretariat* 1992). It contains a lot of advice for the analysis of the local environment in consultation with women. It suggests a combination of techniques drawn from Rapid Rural

Appraisal, a survey method used in Farming Systems Research. It includes interviewing with or without detailed checklists, mapping, modeling, use of aerial photographs, historical calendars, and field trips. Furthermore, the manual provides some case-studies on women's organization, and practical advice on conservation techniques. This may be the most useful practical guide for development workers on the subject so far.

Mary Boesveld (1990) outlines some research questions and a gender methodology for environmental projects. She states that the importance of women's work is often routinely mentioned in development policy and planning, but without a realistic assesment of women's actual work, needs, motivation and limitations as participants in their own right. There is also little systematic research in differences between men and women in access to and use of natural resources. She gives a short checklist with important indicators of women's work and living conditions. Among the indicators: property and usufructury rights, participation in community decision-making structures and knowledge and experience concerning their environment. (see also *Boesveld* in *Rodda* 1991).

Dianne Rocheleau's "multiple user approach" (1987, 1990) may be valuable for assessing the use of land and other natural resources. An important criterium to distinguish the population is "multiple use" and "multiple users" of resources. She distinguishes types of landusers by activity, by tenure (ownership/terms of access) and by unit of organization. To this she adds the distinction between men and women, between age groups and classes of households. These different categories are often involved differently in the management of natural resources. For this Rocheleau has made the distinction between labour input, responsibility and control concerning natural resources (1987). These criteria may be very useful for researchers and planners to gain insight in the complex local reality. E.g. poor women may seem to have autonomy over certain agricultural processes, but often only labor input and responsibility are concerned and not the most crucial: control.

I have come across little participatory tools on the issue. WEDO (the Women's Environment and Development Organization) has developed the "community report cards", an easy tool for people to evaluate the well-being of their own community (neigbourhood, village, or larger scale) in four areas of everyday life. These are: the natural environment, political systems, social priorities and human development. The idea is that people fill in the cards and send them back to WEDO, but one could wonder if the tool is not a bit too vague to be useful (*WEDO* 1992-1).[4]

Researching indigenous knowledge
An important issue in developing a GED methodology is the attention for and strengthening of farmers' experiments and indigenous technological knowledge. Writers emphasising indigenous knowledge, and elaborating on participatory research and technology development *(Chambers et al.* 1989-1,[5] *Haverkort et al./ILEIA* 1991-2 etc.) often have not incorporated gender concerns. *Rocheleau* (1991) argues that the serious attempt to deal with indigenous (ecological) science is likely to obscure half of it. Incorporating (women's) indigenous knowledge in the existing way of practicing science and planning could easily be interpreted as turning the flow of information around from the bottom to the top. This would result in the appropriation of knowledge by scientists, rather than the empowerment of women's ecological science.[6] She points out different ways of arriving at knowledge. For example, she herself has made use of narrative accounts in recording experiences at the interface of two knowledge systems; of indigenous women and men on the one hand and of researchers on the other. Her case from Kenia illustrates that indigenous ecological knowledge extends well beyond strict botanical and agricultural knowledge; it also includes knowledge of environmental history and practical political economy.[7] She states that this kind of research with rural women can "buy time" and "create space" for them to take stock of the larger scale processes which jeopardize ecological, economic and cultural diversity in their rural landscape *(Rocheleau* 1991). Gender aware strengthening of farmers' experiences may be a promising approach in addressing local and large scale factors in the meantime, moving beyond the idea of "dealing with practical problems first". Two other authors writing on women's knowledge systems are Maria Fernandez, and Janice Jiggins, both to be found in *Poats et al.* (1988).

Integrated planning
Caren Levy (1992) outlines a first conceptual framework to integrate gender with environment in development planning. In both separately developed fields of planning, it has been common practice to create checklists. She criticizes this "checklist approach" for its absence of a justification to ask specific questions. They can always be adapted to the goals of the development agency itself. Also, different checklists often

bear no relation to each other. A first step would be to define sustainable development much more clearly. Both gender and environment are socially constructed, and thus both space and time specific. Furthermore, both represent a set of power relations and find their expression in a range of institutions in society. As such, she states, they (institutionalized gender and environment hvdh) are resistant to changes not beneficial to the powerful. Planned intervention is thus only a marginal vehicle for change next to powerful socio-economic and political forces. Levy identifies four key spheres in which actions to challenge the women and environment sector approaches must take place: the political, the technical, the organizational and research spheres. She points out the fact that a gender and environment competence among professionals is no substitute for consultation of and participation by women and men themselves.

Role of intellectuals
Joke Schrijvers (1993) outlines a "transformative approach" to development, in which the researcher serves as an intellectual middle(wo)man in a transformative process from below. This implies a personal, conscious choice of whom one wants to work for and with, which means leaving the dichotomy between the personal and the scientific behind. Although the power relations in present development research make it very difficult, knowledge should be generated in an interactive process between the researcher and the researched, in which cooperation and sharing of responsibility are crucial. *Peggy Antrobus* (1989) feels researchers need to recognize the differences between theories aiming at maintaining the status quo and those that promote social change. In research, one should link micro- and macrolevel analysis, integrate social, cultural and political dimensions into economic analysis, recognize the political nature of development, and be non-dualistic.

Besides its recommendations for policy makers, governments and corporations, the *Global Assembly* report (1992-1) also addresses academia with a number of recommendations. These are:
1 Promote the most salient indicators for monitoring and assesing the interrelationship between women and environment.
2 Develop guidelines and implementation strategies based on experience and dialogue.
3 Continue to carry out interdisciplinary research leading to dialogue, policy formulation and action.

4 Develop linkages with international and NGO communities, to strengthen their environmental capacities.

5 Take cultural diversity into account in integrating gender issues into environmental curricula, research and other priorities.

Recommendations 2, 3, and 4 emphasize the fact that an important goal of every GED methodology should be the strengthening of grass roots inititatives to counteract processes leading to environmental degradation and pollution. The next chapter addresses these initiatives.

Notes

1 Comparable is the conceptual framework of *Feldstein and Poats* (1989), which is included in the *VENAreader* (1991).

2 It may be holistic in the sense that it investigates relations of e.g. a crop with its environment, but FSR/E may be used to investigating only this crop option without recognition of the wider social and political environment of a farming system (see also earlier footnote belonging to 2.2) The dynamic aspects of a farming system, its development in history are not necessarily incorporated in FSR/E research.

3 In *Poats et al* (1988) useful contributions are written by Norem with an overview of existing projects; and Evans who gives a dynamic household model.

4 In this respect it may be useful to contact the International Women's Tribune Center in New York, which has an up to date database on training materials.

5 Although *Chambers* (1985) mentions the male research bias.

6 As argued *Rosemary Jommo* in 5.2.

7 Note also *Melissa Leach's* "micro political economy from a gender perspective" *(Leach* 1991-1).

CHAPTER 8

Countervailing movements and organizations

Most GED literature emphasizes the countervailing actions women undertake against environmental degradation. Very often examples such as the Chipko Movement in India, and the Green Belt Movement in Kenia (see below) are referred to. Here, specific examples will not be discussed, the focus is rather on analytical studies of the movement. In the first paragraph literature is discussed which addresses the combined environmental and women's movements. Special reference is made to India, because of the abundance of publications that have appeared. In the second paragraph, the reader is referred to some publications containing many useful case-studies.

8.1 Analyzing the movements

India
Movements in the South often have an advantage over those in the North; they are more sensitive to relations between various issues. Movements in the South often link issues of poverty, indigenous peoples' and women's issues, environmental destruction and consumer issues. Northern movements tend to be more single issue oriented.

Probably most is written on India. Here traditional agricultural systems are defended by social movements with impressive popular protest actions. They tend to advocate the ban of national, in favour of local resource use *(Haüsler and Charkiewicz-Pluta* 1991-1). *Ramachandra Guha* (1991) locates Himalayan peasant struggles within the context of other anti-colonial movements and customary rebellions in monarchies (including Chipko, see next paragraph).

As discussed earlier *Bina Agarwal* (1989) points out that in India, women's militancy in grassroots resistance is much more linked to family survival than men's. Women fight for social and cultural improvement ("their struggle is not just for bread, but also for dignity"). Women implicitly attempt to search for an alternative existence, based on equality and cooperation. This implies that their struggles are often seen as ecofeminist struggles. An example is given by *Gail Omvedt* (1992), who talks about "ecofeminism in action" in her article, describing the struggles for democracy and environmental sustainability of Indian women, who suffer the triple oppression of caste, class and gender. She sketches the differences between urban and rural activists. Urban feminist groups have provided a theoretical basis for fights against the specific exploitation of women, dealing with issues like violence against women, and home labour. Rural women focus more on political and economic issues (women's land rights for instance). They demand an alternative "people's" brand of development, that must be ecologically sustainable and committed to a rural-centred agroindustrial society. Such turns to alternative production are not a step backward to traditional society, *Omvedt* states. The women activists are rather responding with feminist interpretations of Indian traditions. Culture thus is an integral part of the economic and ecological struggles by rural Indian feminists.

Vandana Shiva (1988-1, 1989, 1991-2 discussed in chapters 2 and 3, see also *Bandyopadhyay & Shiva* 1987) and *Gabrielle Dietrich* (1988 1-3 see chapter 3) have elaborated on the Indian women's ecological movement. Especially noteworthy is the Indian grassroots women's magazine *Manushi* which regularly deals with women's environmental struggles. *Kishwar and Vanita* (1984) have made a compilation of articles that have appeared in Manushi during its first five years.

Interconnecting the movements worldwide
Michael Redclift (1987/89) described some major environmental movements in the South. These are essentially livelihood struggles, "recognizing the necessity of sustainable environmental management". The same parallels can be drawn and interconnections made between the women's and environmental movements, as outlined for India above. *Carolyn Merchant* (1980/etc.) sketched the similarities between the ecology and the women's movement. Both criticize the costs of competition, aggression and domination arising from capitalism. *Lezak Shallat* (1990) also connects the women's and environmental movements. Since the Stockholm conference in 1972 the environmental movement has left the more conservationist stance, and moved towards the advocacy of alternative development options. Similar processes of widening the scope of action have occurred in the women's movement, the peace movement and "green" political and consumer movements

around the world, says Shallat. She states that in the past two decades, women have emerged as the promotors of a new type of issue-based social movement. This social movement transcends conventional political ideologies. The approach to social change seeks to converge movements with similar objectives, such as the feminist, peace, and ecology movements. Women's most effective radius of action can be captured with the famous formula "Think Globally, Act Locally" *(Shallat* 1990). In the past years the environmental movement of women has been moving from this local spheres into worldwide networks and into political circles. Therefore, we can add "and Act Globally As Well" to their slogan.

8.2 Case study materials

The Chipko and Green Belt Movements
Most publications on women, gender and the environment contain examples of women's protest against environmental degradation. In this respect, the Chipko movement in India undoubtedly scores highest. It is reported that grassroots women and men hugged trees (Chipko means to hug) and thus prevented loggers from cutting the trees. Women are said to have been the main force behind this successful tactic *(Shiva* 1989, *Dankelman and Davidson* 1988, *Rodda* 1991 *Bandyopadhyay and Shiva* 1987 etc, see index). Instead of retelling its history and success, here I would like to point out the discrepancy between the bulk of writers -all repeating each other, stressing the role of women in the movement, and writers like *Ramachandra Guha* (1991). He states that women were the activists only in one village, but elsewhere it were mainly the men who protested. Despite its widespread coverage in the media, he argues, there was a surprising lack of sociologically informed analysis of the Chipko movement in which the specific historical context was recognized. This lack may even be caused by the widespread attention, because of the assimilation of the movement into modern discourses of feminism or environmentalism! The movement, he states, is in the first place a peasant movement, a defence of traditional rights in the forest, more than an environmental or feminist movement. Therefore he broadened his study to the total peasant movement in a historical context. His analysis may be male-biased; *Omvedt* (1992) feels that this bias is merely caused by the lack of female leadership in the

Chipko Movement (a tendency strenghtened because of international attention?). However, this discrepancy between different views on the Chipko movement may be a warning against the uncritical use of always the same examples as a proof of women's activism, and against taking these examples out of their context. The same might be true for the Green Belt movement in Kenia *(Wangari Maathai* 1984, 1988), which has mobilized more than 30.000 women to plant trees on the edges of public land. The movement addresses women's living conditions and fuelwood scarcity in the meantime. The African caucus on the World Women's Congress proposed to extend the Green Belt movement as an Africa-wide network *(World Women's Congress* 1992). The examples Chipko and Green Belt movement have been very influential to the GED movement. It is however more interesting to document and analyze new examples by now.

Other organizations
The *Global Assembly* (1991 and 1992-1/2) initiated the documention of successfull organizational initiatives of women to combat environmental degradation and to ameliorate livelihoods. Each case is summarized on one page, which makes it difficult to understand the situation. However, more than documenting the situation in detail, what it is all about is the empowerment of women and the strengthening of their own capacity for effective natural resources management. The Global Assembly selected projects which were considered "repeatable, affordable, sustainable and visible". Although this effort is very worthwhile, the danger is that we are left with insufficient analysis of the specific context under which actions or movements succeed. The final report sketches the policy implications of the need to strengthen women's environmental management (1992-1 and 2). Also *Rodda's* (1991) and *Dankelman and Davidson's* books (1988) contain a number of interesting successful case-studies.

Maria Muller and Dorine Plantenga (1987, 1990) discuss organizations in the urban context.[1] They present 9 case-studies on the role of habitat in poor women's daily lives, using a large amount of material. They conclude that policymakers must be more aware of the informal networks that women have created in their quarters. These informal networks function as survival strategies. These networks do not fundamentally strengthen women's position, but they can be a basis for the establishment of formal organizations, that pursue long-term improvements. Formal organization is also needed to prevent women's networks from marginalization after emergency situations have passed. The book gives examples of formal organizations, and outlines the conditions under which they succeed.

Finally, *March and Taggu* (1986) distinguish between active and defensive strategies of informal associations of women. They argue that the associations with active strategies are best equiped' to receive assistance from and be strengthened by development planners.

In the previous chapters of this guide the need to strengthen women's environmental management has been mentioned regularly, and some recommendations were made. An important new feature of the environmental women's movement, concerns the links which emerge between Northern and Southern organizations in international networks. These networks may be well equiped to attract international donors.

In the next and final chapter gaps in information and documentation will be identified, and recommendations for further research and policy made.

Notes

1 A review of the book, and other references for women and urban habitat see *VENA Newsletter* May 1990. I also refer to *Judith Kjellberg Bell* (1991), who, in a guide to literature on gender and urbanization, says that *Brydon and Chant* (1989) would be an excellent introduction to this issue. A detailed resource document for governments, donors and other agencies on the subject of women and shelter is *IYSH* (1987).

CHAPTER 9

Information and documentation: a way forward

Throughout the guide I have mentioned several subjects on which there seems to be a scarcity of literature. This does not imply that there is no literature at all on these subjects, because the focus has been on information available in the Netherlands. Furthermore, the literature research at the basis of this guide has been very broad, and could not be exhaustive on all subjects considered relevant for the understanding of GED.

Often however, there is clearly a lack of information on certain subjects available to an international audience. It may be interesting to systematically put together the experiences on certain issues, and make them widely available. In this section possible gaps in information and documentation are listed and some recommendations are made. The first paragraph will focus on academics and the second on policy-makers, two different groups by and for whom certain strategic information should be developed, ideally not in complete isolation from each other.

But beforehand it should be said (once more) that the crucial point is not so much the number and quality of academic studies carried out, or the degree to which in policy gender and environment are addressed as a special issue, but the creation of space for women's empowerment. Critical to their empowerment is access to the information produced, and the degree to which in the production of this information their knowledge and ideas are integrated. In this process, NGOs and resource centra play an important role.

9.1 Research

As put forward earlier, we may expect much more work on GED theory in the near future. There is a need for a comprehesive attempt to construct a suitable theoretical framework for GED. Thereby the methodological link between theory and practice is crucial. Practice implies the real world of development decisions taken by women and men in their everyday fight to maintain their livelihood, and to cope with and combat environmental destruction and pollution. Practice also means making development policies. These include plans and decisions by governments, the work of development institutions, and the involvement of the commercial sector. Linking theory and practice implies primarily a serious communication between academics, members of grassroots organizations and policy makers. In chapter 7 some publications were presented which may provide guidelines for linking theory and practice, but they are either too unspecific about the environment, too instrumental about women, or a bit too vague. In other words, a lot needs to be done to establish a suitable methodology for dealing with gender and environment in combination, in a way which is benefial for both women and the natural environment. The recommendations formulated by the *Global Assembly* (7.2) focus on the linkage between academia and women's experiences and actions regarding the environment. It may be interesting for academics involved with GED to further work out these recommendations.

Detailed studies needed
Detailed studies should be conducted about the following topics.
- A number of questions should be raised about the functionality and constraints of gender for environmental protection and women's autonomy in traditional societies. For example, does the gendered division of tasks and knowledge ensure the wise management of complex ecosystems in certain contexts? Exactly which aspects of gender define natural resource management? Which advantages and disadvantages does the gendered division of labour and knowledge, decision-making, access and control have both for women's autonomy and environmental management? This analysis can be done by women and men at the grassroots in cooperation with scientific researchers. The gender aspects of indigenous forest communities, and forest users, may be of special interest.
- Legal aspects of gender and natural resource management, such as differential access and control, and how to overcome the barriers require special attention as well.
- How does the strengthening of women's environmental management influence the position of men? What are possibilities and constraints for men as environmental managers? What measures can be taken in order to strengthen their management possibilities, in a way that does

not reconfirm gender inequalities? How can the harmony of both "tracks of development" of men and women be stimulated?
- Then we need to further elaborate on structural links in GED. How are the factors as put forward in 1.1: sexual division of labour, gender ideology and feminization of poverty related to the environment within a possible theoretical framework?
- Finally factors such as nationality, class, caste, age and ethnicity and their relation to gender and environment should be examined. A special case could be gender and health in the urban environment.

Often when the need to address large scale factors is mentioned in the literature this is not very well worked out. In research, the links between local and larger scale factors should be made clear. More specifically:
- How in theory and practice does gender relate to global environmental problems like loss of biodiversity and the greenhouse effect, both as a cause (gender inequality, ideology etc.) and as a result (different effects on women and men?).
- What are the links between global and large scale factors like militarization, political conservatism and religious fundamentalism, and gender and environment on a local scale? Furthermore, what are the precise effects of debt and structural adjustment, of policies on tariffs and trade?
- What are the effects of national development strategies such as industrialization, modernization of agriculture, and militarization?
- What are the consequences of technological development on gender and environment and especially: (how) can technological development serve women's empowerment and wise environmental management in combination?
- Detailed studies on the connection between population, poverty, and the appropriation of resources by foreign countries and Southern elites are required to steer the population-consumption debate with rational and tangible arguments. A prerequisite is that such studies take into account ethical, human rights and gender considerations, and link macro-, meso- and microlevel factors.

Analysis of the movements
What are the methodological implications of ideas such as social ecofeminism (3.3)?
Are the ecofeminist principles of interconnectedness, equality and diversity really the basis of so many Southern grassroots women's fights

for survival, or is this wishful thinking of those who feel positive about this philosophical strand? It may be interesting to analyze the principles, goals, incentives and potential for transformative change of the movements in some detail. Except for the controversies about the movement in India (8.1 and 2) there is not yet any substantial analytical work on the women's environmental movement or gender in the environmental movement. It would be interesting to put together some detailed case-studies and make extensive comparative analyses of them. What, for instance, makes the movement in Brazil so different from that in Kenia? What factors must we compare? What makes a movement successful? Today, the women's environmental movement links up globally. What are the bottlenecks and benefits in establishing these links? In this process, one would expect much more support from the scientific researcher.

It would be useful to better document the history of the international GED movement, in which policy events, trends and evidence in academic research, and activism are compared and combined. For example, what exactly caused women to emphasize environmental issues in Nairobi 1985? And what trends have led towards the effective lobby of UNCED anno 1992?

What does gender, environment and development really mean for different individuals and groups in different countries? What are the consequences for real solidarity? To what extent are such factors as nationality, class, caste, ethnicity, and the different interests they represent, relevant to gender and the environment?

Transformation
So far, it seems that the ideas of DAWN or social ecofeminism fall outside the scope of the daily concerns of people working in development cooperation. It would be interesting to see if social ecofeminism can serve as a basis for the formulation of alternatives to development in which both women and men contribute equally and effectively. In fact, the "Women's Action Agenda 21" and the Declaration of Women *(Pollard et al.* 1992) reflect the ideas of DAWN and ecofeminism on equality, diversity, interconnectedness. But can we translate such ideas into analytical tools or tangible guidelines for action? Would this not be a challenge to marry top-down and bottom-up ideas?

In frameworks on Gender and Development (like *CCIC et al.* 1991) the link with environmental matters is weak. Is it enough to incorporate environmental concerns in Gender and Development frameworks, or is there an urgent need for a total transformation of development efforts? It is clear that a GED manual such as USAID's (Russo et al. 1989), with its highly instrumental way of dealing with women does not serve women's empowerment. Also, the Dutch paper on the environment *(Ministry* 1990) and the *Commonwealth* manual (1991) do not effectively reflect higher goals of addressing women's autonomy and environmental management. As *Adams* (1990) puts it: "The 'greenness' of development planning (...) is to be found not in its concern with ecology or environment per se, but in its concern with control, power and selfdetermination". And this does not only concern the local level.

What, in this respect, does the transformative approach *(Schrijvers* 1993) imply for a GED methodology? Can intellectuals serve as mediators in a transformative process from below? And, to pose a dangerous question, what if that process is not as "green" or as gender-aware as the concerned intellectual would like it to be? There is a need for a methodological framework in which the continous exchange between researcher and researched, different spheres of knowledge and views, theory and practice are ensured. Scientists working and writing on GED theory should not become "purists". They should not work alienated from the daily reality of the "teachers in the field" who may have it all in their heads, but who have no time to write. Scientists working on an issue like GED should try to translate and adapt their findings in dialogue with the people they focus on, politicians, and others involved in the sustainable development effort.

9.2 Policy

There are some questions which seem relevant especially for Dutch and other policy makers.

The UNCED process in 1992 has exposed a remarkable weakness from the "powerful" nations and a remarkable strength from the "powerless" at the grassroots in arriving at concensus on solutions to the world's environmental problems, despite the differences in ideas and priorities.

The question has now become how to deal with the enormeous gap between policy and activism on GED? They speak a different language, and sometimes they seem to be mutually exclusive. For example, despite some effective lobbying, UNCED's "Agenda 21" (*UNCED* 1992-2) and "Women's Action Agenda 21" (*World Women's Congress* 1992), seem to reflect totally different worlds. *WEDO* (1992-2) has made an attempt to translate the women's agenda for policy makers involved with UNCED. These efforts are very worthwhile. Much more documentation on effective translation is recommendable.

Then there is the translation of useful elements in international guidelines into practical measures. How can the proposed objectives and activities for National governments as listed in "Agenda 21" (e.g. chapter 24) be operationalized?

There are discrepancies (or tensions) to overcome between long-term and short-term goals, social and environmental policy, local and international interests, and top-down and bottom-up approaches *(Wieberdink/InDRA* 1992). The issue of knowledge exchange seems to be extremely relevant in this respect.

How, for example, does the transfer of environmental technology from the North to the South (which was much debated in the UNCED process) relate to indigenous environmental technology and gender? There is a large discrepancy between the scale and scope of these two types of "knowledge systems", which has to be overcome. Can the different domains of knowledge be complementary? Which is most useful for a given environmental matter, scale and sphere (e.g. severe pollution needs to be cleaned up by large scale modern technology, the management of a forest may be best in the hands of village people). How can the indigenous knowledge of women and men be combined with modern scientific knowledge in a process of mutual learning, to achieve sustainable development?

Despite the hope one feels when hearing about "success stories", it is relevant to maintain a critical view on projects and movements claiming to benefit both the position of women and the environment. Also critical reviews are needed of the GED rhetoric of governmental and NGO development institutions and its application in practice. Especially, one should be wary of strategies which present and use women as instruments for environmental projects without strengthening their position.

It is a major challenge to outline how women's environmental management and autonomy can be strengthened in combination. This goes beyond the context of development projects, and has to be included into all other spheres of policy and research. For an integrative approach to GED, it is necessary to define the steps to break down the bureaucratic walls between environmental and women's institutions and between departments of national and international matters.

For Northern governments it is necessary to work out the connection between their countries overconsumption and overexploitation on the one hand, and environmental degradation and pollution on the other, and outline the consequences for a coherent sustainable development policy.

Women are underrepresented in decision-making positions, also on the environment. Apart from the point of view of justice and equality, it is often argued that more women representatives will guarantee a more just and ecologically sound policy. It is important to increase the number of women in decision-making positions and study the effect on environmental policy. Who are the lobbyist for gender awareness, and what do they achieve? What are their incentives, possibilities and constraints?

Let us hope that the readers of this guide are not only introduced to the field, but are also inspired to take up some of the questions in their own research, policy-making or daily practice.

PART II

Bibliography on gender, environment and development

Compiled by Heleen van den Hombergh, assisted by Corrie
Wessendorp/InDRA

This bibliography is an alphabetical list of references discussed in the text,
as well as many other publications. One can use the index (page 165 to 176)
to find titles on specific subjects in the bibliography. Behind the title
description one finds a code between brackets, e.g. (VENA), indicating the
libraries in the Netherlands where the publication can be found. (–) means
that the place where the publication can be found is unknown. If no code
is added, the publication can be consulted at InDRA.

The key to the library codes and the location of the magazines are
given (as far as known) on page 160 to 164. Besides the library codes,
reference is made to the pages in the text where the publication is
discussed.

A

Abramovitz, Janet N. and R. Nichols (1992), Women and biodiversity: ancient reality, modern imperative. In: *Development,* No. 2 (1992), pp 85-90

Achterhuis, H.J. (1990), *Van moeder aarde tot ruimteschip: humanisme en milieucrisis.* Inaugurele rede uitgesproken bij de aanvaarding van het ambt van bijzonder hoogleraar in de humanistische wijsbegeerte, in het bijzonder met betrekking tot de relatie mens en natuur, aan de Landbouwuniversiteit te Wageningen op donderdag 29 maart 1990. Fotocopy available (LEEUW) *48*

Adams, W.M. (1992), *People, environment and development: the urgent need for transformation: Sustainable development: a solution to the development puzzle?* (InDRA Lecture Series)

Adams, W.M. (1990), *Green development. Environment and sustainability in the Third World.* London: Routledge ISBN 0-415-00443-8
25, 28, 45, 46, 87, 104

Afshar, Haleh (ed.) (1991), *Women, development and survival in the Third World.* London; New York: Longman. Inc. ISBN 0-58203492-2 (Inst. 323) (VENA)

Agarwal, Anil (1992), Who will help her learn? To keep the girl child in school, the environment must be improved. In: *Down to Earth,* November 15, 1992, pp 22-33

Agarwal, Anil (et al.)/CSE (1991), *The CSE statement on global environmental democracy.* To be submitted to the forthcoming UNCED. New Delhi: Centre for Science and Environment

Agarwal, Anil and Sunita Narain (1989), *Towards green villages, a strategy for environmentally sound and participatory rural development.* New Delhi: Centre for Science and Environment

Agarwal, Anil (et al.) (eds.)/CSE (1987), *The fight for survival: peoples action for environment.* New Delhi: Centre for Science and Environment (Inst. 175)

Agarwal, Anil (1985-1), Domestic air pollution. The effect of wood smoke on the health of Women. In: *Manushi:* a journal about women in society; No. 28, 1985. pp 13-21 (in: reader Schenk-Sandbergen, (1991-1) pp 134-143)

Agarwal, Anil (1985-2), Taboos make hygiene difficult for women. In: *Gate,* No. 4, p 29 (in: reader Schenk-Sandbergen (1991-1) p 226 *72*

Agarwal, Anil and Sunita Narain (1985-3), Women and natural resources. In: *Social Action.* Vol. 35, No. 4, 1985 (Oct./Dec.)

Agarwal, Bina (1989), Rural women, poverty and natural resources.

Sustenance, sustainability and struggle for change. In: *Economic and Political Weekly,* No. 28, 1989 (October) pp 46-65 (in: reader Schenk-Sandbergen pp 1-20)   *35, 95*

Agarwal, Bina (1988-1), *Neither sustenance nor sustainability, agricultural strategies & ecological degradation and Indian women in poverty.* In: Bina Agarwal (ed), "Structures of patriarchy: state, community and household in modernising Asia". Indian association for women's studies. London: Zed Books, 1988 pp 83-120 (Women and the household in Asia; Vol. 2). Fotocopy available (VENA)

Agarwal, Bina (1988-2), Who sows, who reaps? Women and land rights in India. In: *The Journal of Peasant Studies;* Vol. 15, No. 4, 1988 (July) pp 531-581. Fotocopy available   *31*

Agarwal, Bina (1986), *Cold hearths and barren slopes. The woodfuel crisis in the third world.* London: Zed Books. ISBN 0-86232-539-0

"Agenda 21", see UNCED 1992, see UNIFEM 1992

Agenda Ya Wananchi, see ELCI 1992-1 and 2

Aguiar, Neuma (1990), *Political factors in the debt crisis: alternatives from women's perspectives.* In: WIDE Bulletin (special report), No. 1, 1990. pp 6-10. Fotocopy available

Aguiar, Neuma (1988), *The crisis in Latin America and its impact on women: a summary of research by members of the DAWN-Network in Latin America.* In: ISIS/DAWN. "Confronting the crisis in Latin America, women organize for change". (Book Series 1988-2, Santiago, Chile). pp 11-22

Aidoo, Agnes Akosua (1988-1), *Women and environmental rehabilitation.* African Training and Research Centre for Women (ATRCW)/UN Economic Commission for Africa (ECA). Addis Ababa, Ethiopia. Fotocopy available

Aidoo, Agnes (1988-2), Women and food security; the opportunity for Africa. In: *Development:* Journal of the Society for International Development; Vol. 2/3, 1980 pp 53-55

Akeroyd, Anne V. (1991), *Gender, food production and property rights: constraints on women farmers in Southern Africa.* In: Haleh Afshar, "Women, development and survival in the Third World". pp 139-173. Fotocopy available

Alders, J.G.M./UNCED (1991), Minister of housing, physical planning and environment of the Netherlands (1991) *Statement on behalf of the European Community and its member states.* Third session of the Preparatory Committee for the United Nations Conference on Environment and Development, Geneva 12 August - 4 September 1991),

Presidency of the European Communities, Chatelaine, Geneva, par. 11
and 12   79

Allison, Helen (et al.) (eds.) (1986), *Hard cash. Man-made development and its consequences. A feminist perspective on aid.* CHANGE, War on WANT. ISBN 0-907236-19-7

Amstel, A.R. van (et al.) (1987), *Exportlandbouw in de derde wereld en de effecten op natuur en milieu.* Amsterdam: Interfacultaire Vakgroep Milieukunde (UVA). Instituut voor Milieuvraagstukken (VU). (IVAM onderzoeksreeks; No. 25, IVM rapport; R 87/1)

Anand, Anita (1983), *Saving trees, saving lives, Third World women and the issue of survival.* In: Leonie Caldecott and Stephanie Leland (ed). "Reclaim the earth, women speak out for life on earth". London: The Women's Press. pp 182-187

Andruss, Van (et al.) (eds.) (1990), *Home! A bioregional reader.* Philadelphia etc: New Society Publishers. ISBN USA 0-86571-188-7 / ISBN Canada 1-55092-007-3   52

Antrobus, Peggy (1992), *Speech for "Vrouwenberaad Ontwikkelingssamenwerking"*, 27 maart 1992 in Utrecht. (extensive summary and discussion of speech about DAWN)   43

Antrobus, Peggy (1991-1), *Women's networking and participation: North/South: the DAWN Network.* Presentation at the 20th World Conference of the Society for International Development Global Seminar II: Towards a strategy for growth, sustainability and solidarity: public and private responsibilities, May 6-9, 1991, Amsterdam   43, 44

Antrobus, Peggy (1991-2), Disarmament, peace and solidarity in the changing world order: a woman's vision. In: *Development,* Journal of the Society for International Development. Vol. 1, 1991. p 79

Antrobus, Peggy (1991-3), *The real world for women: political, educational and cultural.* Testimony for the World Women's Congress for a Healthy Planet, Nov. 8-12, 1991, Miami   33

Antrobus, Peggy (1989), Women and development: an alternative analysis. In: *Development,* Journal of the Society for International Development. Vol. 1, 1989. pp 26-28 (also in: InDRA reader '91-2)   44, 93

Appleton, S. (1991), Gender dimensions of structural adjustment: the role of economic theory and quantitative analyses. In: *IDS Bulletin.* Vol. 22, No. 1. pp 13-23

Arias, Margarita (1991), *It's time for women to mother earth:* keynote speech for the World Women's Congress for a Healthy Planet, Nov. 8-12, 1991, Miami

Armstrong, Liz and Adrienne Scott/WEED Foundation (1992), *Whitewash.*

*Exposing the health and environmental dangers of women's sanitary
products and disposable diapers.* Toronto: Harper Collins/(Women and
Environments Education and Development Foundation)   *61*
Arnold, E., see Faulkner, W. & E. Arnold
Arts, Bas en Andrea Berghuizen (1992), Duurzame ontwikkeling
uitgekleed. Theorie en praktijk van UNCED. In: *Derde Wereld* 92-2 pp
49-76
                                                              24, 44, 45
Arts, Bas and Mirjam van Reisen (1988), (Boek)bespreking: vrouwen en
milieu. In: *Derde Wereld,* 88-3 (Boekenrubriek) pp 80-85   *30*
Aryee, Gloria (SWAG-Ghana) (1989), *Case study: food and energy self
sufficiency project, Ghana.* Women and environment seminar. DAC
Expert Group on Women in Development
Asseldonk, H. van and R. Boersma (1987), *Ecofeminisme en de overheersing
van vrouw en natuur in de landbouw.* Zomeruniversiteit Vrouwenstudies
Groningen. (LEEUW)

B
Bakhteari, Quratul Ain (1988), Building on traditional patterns for women
empowerment at grassroots level. In: *Development,* Journal of the
Society for International Development. Vol. 4, 1988. pp 55-60. Fotocopy
available
Bandyopadhyay, J. and Vandana Shiva (1987), Chipko: rekindling India's
forest culture. In: *The Ecologist: the journal of the post industrial age.*
Vol. 1, No. 1. 1987 (also in: InDRA reader '91-'92). Fotocopy available
                                                                  96, 97
Barten, Francoise (1992), *Environmental lead exposure of children in
Managua, Nicaragua: an urban health problem.* Een wetenschappelijke
proeve op het gebied van de Medische Wetenschappen. (Proefschrift
Nijmegen) ISBN 90-9005146-5   *71*
Baxter, Diana (1981), *Women and the environment.* Sudan Institute of
Environmental Studies, University of Khartoum. (Environmental
Research paperseries; No. 2) (ISS/VENA)
Bennett, Olivia (ed.) (1991), *Greenwar: environment and conflict.* By Nafissa
Abdel Rahim, Tafesse Hailu et al. London etc: Panos Publications Ltd.
ISBN 1-870670-23-X   *65*
Berg, Majoos van den (1990), Groene vrouwen op de bres voor het milieu.
Feministische milieu-activistes. In: *Wetenschap & Samenleving,* jrg 42,
no. 4, 1990. pp 29-32
Berghuizen, Andrea:, see Arts, Bas en Andrea Berghuizen

Bernstein, Henry (ed.) (et al.) (1990) *The food question: profits versus people?*
London: Earthscan Publications Ltd. ISBN 1-85383-063-1   *66*
Bertell, Rosalie (1991), *Testimony* for the World Women's Congress for a
Healthy Planet (International Institute of Concern for Public Health),
Nov. 8-12, 1991, Miami   *64, 71*
Beye, I. (1989), *Food for the future: correcting enduring agricultural errors for
achieving future food security.* Report of a workshop on sustainable
agriculture, Nairobi. Kenya: Environmental Liaison Centre
Bhasin, Kamla (et al.) (ed.) (1991), *Our indivisible environment. A report of
the FAO-FFHC/(FAO-Freedom From Hunger Campaign and Action for
Development) Workshop on South Asian Environmental Perspective.*
Bangalore October 1-7, 1990. New Delhi: Design and Print   *33*
Bhatt, Ela (1989), Article about SEWA (Self-Employed Women's
Association). In: *World development.* Vol. 17, No. 7, 1989. pp 1059-1065
(Inst. 310)
Bicocci, Cynthia Gay & Kathleen H. Ochs (bibliography) (1990), *Women
and technology: an annotated research guide.* New York: Garland
Publishing. (IIAV)   *63*
Bij, Rinske van der (1991), Een wereld van verschil: schrijven of werken aan
autonomie voor vrouwen. In: *Derde Wereld.* Jrg. 9, No. 5, 1991
(Februari). pp 10-14   *57*
Birke, Lynda (1986), *Women, feminism and biology. The feminist challenge.*
Brighton; Wheatsheaf (Inst. 264)   *49*
Blaikie, Piers, and Harold Brookfield (1987), *Land degradation and society.*
London and New York: Routledge. (Development studies) ISBN
0-415-06597-6   *46, 87*
Boersma, R., see Asseldonk, H van and R. Boersma
Boesveld, Mary (1990), *Planning with women for wise use of the
environment. Research and practical issues.* In: M. Marchand and H.A.
Udo de Haes (ed.) "The people's role in wetland management"
proceedings of the International Conference on Wetlands, the
Netherlands, Leiden, 5-8 June 1989. pp 781-790. Fotocopy available
(book also available)   *91*
Boesveld, Mary (1986), *Towards autonomy for women. Research and action to
support a development process.* The Hague: RAWOO (Working paper; No.
1) (VENA)
Boesveld, M., see also Postel, E. en M. Boesveld
Boetes, M. (1990), Emancipatie en milieu: Gemiste kans? In: *A Propos.* No.
3, 1990 (derde kwartaal). pp 2-4   *86*
Bokdam, Carla (1988), *Vrouwen en milieuproblematiek in rurale gebieden in*

de Derde Wereld; twee visies. Derde Wereld Centrum, Katholieke
Universiteit Nijmegen; Werkgroep "Milieu en Onderontwikkeling"

Bonsink, Hilda (1989), *Vrouwen en habitat. Woonomstandigheden en
genderbehoeften van vrouwen in volksbuurten van grote Derde
Wereldsteden.* Amsterdam: Vrije Universiteit, Vakgroep Culturele
Antropologie/Sociologie der Niet-Wetsterse Samenlevingen.
(Feministische Antropologie; No. 3)   *40*

Bookchin, M (1990), *Remaking society: pathways to a green future.* Boston:
South End Press. ISBN 0-89608372-1 (ISS) (Inst. 126)   *52, 54*

Borg, Brigitte van der/FAO (1989), *Introduction to the reader on women's role
in forest resource management.* Regional wood. In: Women's role in
forest resource management: a reader / Prepared by Brigitte van der
Borg. (Regional wood energy development programme in
Asia-GCP/RAS/131/NET) (Project Working Paper No. 1) Bangkok: FAO,
1989. pp 1-7

Boserup, Esther (1970/1989), *Woman's role in economic development.*
London: Earthscan Publications Ltd. 2nd ed. (edition 1970: New York:
St. Martin's Press) ISBN 1-85383-040-2   *23, 39, 57*

Both Ends (1992), *Report of the meeting of coordinators of international
networks on women, environment and development.* Amsterdam 8-10
October 1992. Amsterdam: Both Ends

Bowles, Regine (1989), *De rechten van vrouwen op land in Kenya.*
Doctoraalscriptie Nederlands Recht, Faculteit der Rechtsgeleerdheid
Rijks Universiteit Groningen. (Both Ends)

Brah, M., see Monimart, Marie and M. Brah

Braidotti, Rosi (et al.) (1993), *Women, environment and sustainable
development: towards a theoretical synthesis.* London: Zed Books. ISBN
1-85649-184-6   *37, 63*

Briones, Leonor M./Freedom from Debt Coalition, Phillipines (1991),
Debt, poverty, maldevelopment and misallocation of resources. Testimony
for World Women's Congress for a Healthy Planet, Nov. 8-12 1991,
Miami   *60*

Briscoe, John (1986), *Water supply and health in developing countries: selected
primary health care revisited.* In: Joseph S. Tulchin (ed), "Habitat,
Health and development. A new way of looking at cities in the Third
world". Colorado: Lynne Rienner Publications. pp 105-120 (in: reader
Schenk-Sandbergen, 1991-2 pp 231-241)

Brookfield, Harold, see Blaikie, Piers and Harold Brookfield

Brouwer, Christien (et al.) (1992), Bibliografie natuur en milieu. In: *Lover,*
92-3, pp 190-193   *49*

Brouwer, Christien (1990), Hierarchie of harmonie? Gender en de
wetenschappelijke benadering van de natuur. In: *Tijdschrift voor
vrouwenstudies.* Vol. 11, No. 11 (1990) 43-3, pp 260-271   *49*
Brown, Lester R. (et al.) (1993), *State of the world 1993: a Worldwatch
Institute report on progress toward a sustainable society.* New York;
London: W.W. Norton & Company. ISBN 0-393-30963-0
Brown, Rosemary (1991), Matching women, environment and development
around the world. In: *Women and Environments.* Vol. 13, No. 2, 1991. pp
37-41   *35, 49, 66*
Brown, Valerie A. and Margaret A. Switzer (1991), *Women and ecologically
sustainable development. Engendering the debate.* A discussion paper for
consideration by the ESD Working Groups. Australian National
University, for the Office of the Status of Women, Department of the
Prime Minister and Cabinet   *71, 86*
Bruyn, Milly de (1992), *GATTing greener. A paper on trade and the
environment.* Masters thesis Leiden University Department of
International Law (Milieudefensie)
Brydon, L. and S. Chant (ed.) (1989), *Women in the Third World: gender
issues in rural and urban areas.* New Brunswick: Rutgers University
Press. ISBN 0-8135-1471-1   *99*
Büchner, Gregor (et al.) (1990), *Gender, environmental degradation and
development: the extent of the problem.* (Paper of the "Environment and
Development Seminar", at University College London in 1990).
London: London Environmental Economics Centre. 37p   *57, 58*
Bushwick, Nancy (1985), Women and the environment, seeing the linkages
in economic development. In: *Ecoforum.* Vol. 10, No. 2, 1985 (April). p 3
(LUW)

C

Caldecott, Leonie and Stephanie Leland (eds.) (1983), *Reclaim the earth:
women speak out for life on earth.* London: The women's press. (–)   *50*
Caldicott, H. (1992), *If you love this planet: a plan to heal the earth.* New
York; London: W.W. Norton & Company. ISBN 0-393-30835-9
Campen, Marlou van (1988), *Overleven op gif: een onderzoek onder actieve
bewoonsters van gebieden met bodemverontreiniging.* Doctoraalscriptie
Landbouwuniversiteit Wageningen, Vakgroep Sociologie.
(Milieudefensie)
Carson, Rachel (1962), *Silent Spring.* Cambridge Mass.: Riverside Press.
(Reprinted in 1977, Harmondsworth, Middlesex: Penguin Books. ISBN
0-14002268-6 (Inst. 264) (Centrale Bibliotheek Wageningen)   *24, 64, 71*

Canadian Council for International Cooperation, see CCIC
Castleton, Dulce, see Dennis, Francis and Dulce Castleton/DAC/Expert
Group on Women in Development

CCIC (et al.) (1991), *Two halves make a whole. Balancing gender relations in development.* Ottawa: Canadian Council for International Coöperation
38, 41, 89, 103

CCIC (1990), *Environmental screening of NGO development projects.* Ottawa: Canadian Council for International Coöperation

Cecelski, Elisabeth (1987-1), Energy and rural women's work: Crisis, response and policy alternatives. In: *International Labour Review.* 126, No. 1, 1987 (Jan.-Feb.). Fotocopy available   *75*

Cecelski, Elisabeth/ILO (1987-2) *Linking energy with survival: a guide to energy, environment and rural women's work.* Geneva: ILO (LEEUW) (VENA)
69, 75

Cecelski, E. (1986), *Energy and rural women's work: Geneva 21-25 October, 1985.* Technical cooperation Report, Geneva: ILO 1986, ISBN 92-2-105466-7 & 92-2-105519-1. Vol. I: Proceedings of preparatory meeting on energy and rural women's work. Vol. II: Papers of a prep ... (ARBOR)

CEFEMINA, see Trejos, Marta/CEFEMINA

Centre for Our Common Future, see Starke, Linda/The Centre for Our Common Future

Chakraborty, Manab, see Wadehra, Renu and Manab Chakraborty

Chambers, Robert and Gordon R. Conway (1991), *Sustainable rural livelihoods: practical concepts for the 21st century.* ISBN 0-9037-15-458-9 (Discussion Paper IDS-D 296)

Chambers, Robert (et al.) (eds.) (1989-1). *Farmer first. Farmer innovation and agricultural research.* London: Intermediate Technology Publications. ISBN 1-85339-007-0   *92*

Chambers, Robert (et al.) (1989-2), *To the hands of the poor: water and trees.* London: Intermediate Technology Publications. ISBN 1-85339-047-x

Chambers, Robert (1988), *Sustainable rural livelihoods: a key strategy for people, environment and development.* In: Czech Conroy and Miles Litvinoff (ed), "The greening of aid, sustainable livelihoods in practice". pp 1-17   *46*

Chambers, Robert (1985), *The Working Women's Forum: a counter-culture by poor women.* New Delhi: UNICEF Regional Office for South Central Asia   *94*

Chant, S., see Brydon, L. and S. Chant

Charkiewicz-Pluta, Ewa (1993), *Women, the environment and development:*

in search of tools for social and ecological transformation. Draft for the Lecture Series at the University of Amsterdam, organised by InDRA. "People, environment and development", January 14th, 1993   *68*

Charkiewicz-Pluta, Ewa, see also Haüsler, Sabine and Ewa Charkiewicz-Pluta

Cheney, Jim (1987), Eco-feminism and deep ecology. In: *Environmental Ethics*. Vol. 9, No. 2, 1987 (Summer). pp 115-145. Fotocopy available

Chimedza, Ruvimbo (1989), *Women, natural resource management and household food security:* an overview. Harare: Department of Agricultural Economics and extension, University of Zimbabwe (Working Paper AAE 1/89)   *72*

China Environment News, see Weimin, Chen/China Environment News

Chinery-Hess, M (ed.) (1989), *Engendering adjustment for the 1990-s.* London: Commonwealth Secretariat Publications (VENA)

Chitepo, Victoria (1991), Population, women and the environment. In: *Development*, Journal of the Society for International Development. Vol. 1, 1991 "Reflections on Global Solidarity: One World or Several". pp 124-128

Chowdhry, Kamla (1989), Poverty, environment, development. Comments on Kamla Chowdry's essay. In: *Daedalus*, Journal of the American Academy of Arts and Sciences. 1989 (winter). Issue: "A World to make: Development in Perspective". pp 141-158 (Inst. 173/264). Fotocopy available

Clones, Julia/World Bank (1991), *Women's crucial role in managing the environment in Sub-Sahara Africa*. Technical Note, Women in Development, Poverty and Social Policy Division, Technical Department Africa Region   *18, 81, 82*

Cobb, John B., see Daly, Herman E. and John B. Cobb

Cockburn, Alexander, see Hecht, Susanna and Alexander Cockburn

Colby, Michael E. (1989), *The evolution of paradigms of environmental management in development*. Paper (World Bank), 1989 (October). Fotocopy available   *47*

Collard, Andree and Joyce Contrucci (1988), *Rape of the wild. Man's violence against animals and the earth*. Bloomington: Indiana university Press. ISBN 0-253-20519-0   *50*

Collins, Joseph, see Lappé, Frances Moore and Joseph Collins

Commissie Ecologie en Ontwikkelingssamenwerking/Commission Ecology and Development Cooperation (1986-1, 2, 3) *Environment and development cooperation 1. Advice 2. Documentation 3. Explanation.*

Amsterdam: Koninklijk Instituut voor de Tropen/Royal Tropical
Institute. English version as appendix to Dutch Version   *83*
Commonwealth Secretariat (1992), *Women, conservation and agriculture: a
manual for trainers*. London: Commonwealth Secretariat; Women and
Development Programme; Human Resource Development Group *90,104*
Conroy, Czech and Miles Litvinoff (ed.) (1988), *The greening of aid,
sustainable livelihoods in practice*. London: IIED, Earthscan Publishers
Ltd. ISBN 1-85383-016-X   *46*
Concerned Scholars, see DAWN/Concerned Scholars
Consumers Association of Penang, Malaysia, see Hong,
Eveline/Consumers Association of Penang, Malaysia
Contrucci, Joyce, see Collard, Andree and Joyce Contrucci
Conway, Gordon R., see Chambers, Robert and Gordon R. Conway
Corral, Thais (1991), *Women and environment in Brasil: a new label for old
problems*. Paper for panel discussion Women, Environment and
Development, Both Ends/Ipac steering committee May 31, Amsterdam,
the Netherlands
Costello, A. (et al.) (1989), *The sanitary protection scandal*. London: The
Women's Environmental Network. (Milieudefensie)   *61*
Council of Europe (1988), "Symposium on women's voice in the
North-South dialogue. Strategies for interdependence and solidarity,
Barcelona 30-31 May 1988", European Public Campaign on North-south
interdependence and solidarity, Strasbourg '88 *Introduction, conclusions
of the panel on ecological interdependence, report of the panel on
socio-cultural interdependence*. Fotocopy available
Court, Thijs de la (1992), *Different worlds: development cooperation beyond
the nineties*. Utrecht: International Books; Jan van Arkel. ISBN
90-6224-996-5
Court, Thijs de la (1991), *Critique of the dominant development paradigm
from a deep ecology view and from a radical feminist view*. Paper for the
workshop on Women, the Environment and Sustainable Development:
Towards a theoretical framework, May 28, 1991. The Hague: Institute of
Social Studies   *52, 86*
Court, Thijs de la (1990), *Beyond Brundtland; Green development in the
1990's*. London: Zed Books. ISBN 0-86232-905-1   *86*
Creevy, L.D. (ed.) (1986), *Woman farmers in Africa, rural development in
Mali and the Sahel*. New York: Syracuse, N.Y. Syracuse University Press
(VENA)
CSE (1991), *Floods, flood plains and environmental myths*, State of India's

Environment, A Citizens Report 3. New Delhi: Centre for Science and Environment. (ASC)

CSE (1985), *Women and natural resources.* In: "State of India's Environment. Second Citizens Report '84-'85." Delhi: Center for Science and Environments. pp 172-188. Fotocopy available

CSE, see also Agarwal, Anil (et al.)/CSE

D

DAC/Expert group on Women in Development, see Moser, Caroline/DAC/Expert Group on Women in Development, see Dennis, Francis and Dulce Castleton/DAC/Expert Group on Women in Development

DAC/OECD (1990), *Focus on the future: women and environment.* London: IIED

DAC/OECD (1988), *Women and the environment.* (submitted by the DAC Expert Group on Women in Development) Paris: OECD (Room Document; No. 3)   55, 60

DAC/WID Expert group task force (1988) *Women and environment.* Discussion paper for the DAC/WID expert group task force

Dahl, G. (ed.) (1987), *Woman in pastoral production,* Stockholm: Ethnographical Museum of Sweden. (LEEUW)

Dahlberg, Frances (ed.) (1981), *Woman the gatherer.* New Haven and London: Yale University Press. ISBN 0-300-02989-6

Daly, Herman E. and John B. Cobb (1989), *For the common good. Redirecting the economy towards the community, the environment and a sustainable future.* Boston: Beacon Press (Both Ends)

Daly, Mary (1978/1984), *Gyn/ecology, the metaethics of radical feminism.* London: Women's Press. ISBN 0-704-33850-5 (Inst. 177/126)

DANIDA (1987), *Cross-cutting dimensions in DANIDA evaluation reports: sustainability, women and environment* / Hannov Nezo Jensen, Hans Otto Sano. Ed. Knud Svendsen. Copenhagen: Centre for Development Research

Dankelman, Irene (1991-1), *Women, children and environment: implications for sustainable development.* Paper for "Women and Children First" Symposium on the impact of environmental degradation and poverty on women and children, Geneva, 27-30 May 1991. Conches: UNCED Secretariat   19, 55, 62, 69, 73

Dankelman, Irene, and Vandana Shiva (1991-2), *Women and girls maintaining the food chain. A casestudy on gender and biodiversity in Garhwal (north India)*   73

Dankelman, Irene (1991-3), Sustainable development: the gender perspective. In: *Development,* Journal of the Society of International Development. Vol. 1, 1991 "Reflections on Global Solidarity: One World or Several". pp 134-135

Dankelman, Irene and Joan Davidson (1988), *Women and environment in the Third World: alliance for the future.* London: Earthscan in association with IUCN (second edition, 1989). (The IUCN sustainable development series). ISBN 1-85383-003-8   *18, 19, 24, 29, 54, 55, 69, 71, 73, 77, 97, 98*

Dankelman, Irene (1987), *Women in the Brundtland Report* (note) 2p. ICDA Special report September 1987. In: "IUCN 1987-2 IUCN Workshop on Women and the World Conservation Strategy"   *78*

Dasgupta, Sugata (1985), The population explosion and development: some myths, fallacies and remedies. In: *Praxis,* a quarterly journal, 1985. New Delhi: People's institute for Development and Training. pp 70-97. Fotocopy available

Datta, Satya (ed.) (1990), *Third World urbanization: reappraisals and new perspectives.* Stockholm: Swedish Council for Research in the Humanities and Social Sciences. (KIT)

David, Rosalind (1991), *Food security and the environment: a select annotated bibliography.* Sussex: IDS. (Development Bibliography Series; 4) ISBN 0-903-35493-4 / ISSN 0955-0569

Davidson, Joan (1990), *Women and the environment,* paper 3 WAMM 90/IV/(ii). Third Meeting of Commonwealth Ministers Responsible for Women's Affairs, Ottawa, Canada 9-12 October 1990   *19*

Davidson, Joan (1989), Restoring women's link with nature. In: *Earthwatch.* No. 37, 1989. pp 2-3   *19*

Davidson, Joan, see also Dankelman, Irene and Joan Davidson

Davies, Katherine (1988), What is ecofeminism? In: *Women and environments.* 1988 (Spring). In: ISIS International 1991 (information pack)

Davies, Katherine (1987), Historical associations: women and the natural world. In: *Women and Environments.* 1987 (Spring). In: ISIS International 1991 (information pack)

Davies, S. and Melissa Leach (eds.) (1991), *Food security and the environment: conflict or compementarity.* (D 285 IDS discussion paper, Sussex, ISBN 0903715 392, or *IDS Bulletin* 22:3)

Davis, D.L. and J.H. Nadel (eds.) (1988), *To work and to weep, women in fishing societies.* St. John's: ISER, Memorial University of New Foundland. (–)

Davis, Donald Edward (1989), *Ecophilosophy. A field guide to the literature.* California: Peace and Plenty (Both Ends)   47

Davis, Kathy (et al.) (1991), *The gender of power.* London (etc): SAGE. ISBN 0-80398542-8 (VENA) (Inst. 315)

Davison, H. (ed.) (1988), *Agriculture, women and land: the African experience,* Boulder (etc.): Westview Press. ISBN 0-8133-7421-9 (LEEUW)

DAWN/Concerned Scholars (1992), *Policy statement on population and the environment.* By: Concerned Scholars participating in an SSRC/ISSC/DAWN. Workshop on Population and the Environment. Mexico, Jan./Feb. 1992

DAWN (1991), *Alternatives.* Vol. 1. The Food, Energy and Debt Crises in Relation to Women. Rio de Janeiro: Editora Rosa dos Tempos

DAWN, see also Sen, Gita and Caren Grown/DAWN

Dehlot, Colette (1991), *Managers of natural resources.* Section of: Rodda, 1991. pp 72-78   73, 74

Dennis, Francis and Dulce Castleton/DAC/Expert Group Women in Development, *Women's mobilization in human settlements. Case study: the Guarari housing project, Costa Rica.* (paper for the "Women and environment seminar" – DAC Expert Group on Women in Development) 12p

Deval, B & G. Sessions (1985), *Deep ecology, living as if nature mattered.* Layton, Utah: Peregine, Smith Books (ISS)   47

Development Alternatives with Women for a New Area, see DAWN

Development, issue (1989), Special issue 1989; 2/3 eg C.Y. Ling, WED: the Malaysian Experience, A.M. Paul, WED: case studies from Ghana

Dey, Jenny (1984), *Women in rice farming systems.* Science and Public Policy Journal of the Science Policy Foundation, issue on "women in Third World Agriculture", Vol. 11, No. 4, 1984 (August) pp 201-218

DGIS, see Ministry of Foreign Affairs

Diamond, Irene and Gloria F. Orenstein (edited and with essays by) (1990), *Reweaving the world; the emergence of ecofeminism.* San Fransisco: Sierra Club Books. ISBN 0-87156-623-0   50, 52, 71

Dietrich, Gabriele (1990), *Women and housing rights.* NCHR Workshop-New Delhi- March 1990

Dietrich, Gabriele (1989), *Development debate/ models & gender implications.* Zending en Wereld Diakonaat 90/253 1989. Fotocopy available   49

Dietrich, Gabriele (1988-1), *Women's movement in India: conceptual and religious reflections.* (selected essays). Bangalore: Breakthrough Publications   96

Dietrich, Gabriele (1988-2), *Women, ecology and culture.* In: "Women's

Movement in India, Conceptual and Religious Reflections". Bangalore: Breakthrough Publications. pp 150-173   *31, 49, 96*

Dietrich, Gabriele (1988-3) *Development, ecology and women's struggles.* In: "Women's Movement in India, Conceptual and Religious Reflections". Bangalore: Breakthrough Publications. pp 174-186   *96*

Direktion fur Entwicklungszusammenarbeit und Humanitare Hilfe (1990), *Femmes et environnement, nouvelles evidences, nouveaux defis pour le developpement.* Bern, Suisse

Documento aprobado por la plenaria del encuentro internacional mujer y medio ambiente en America Latina y el Caribe (1990), Quito, 19-22 Marzo (first meeting women and environment in lat. am)

Doorenbos, J. (et al.) (1988), Women and the rationalisation of smallholder agriculture. In: *Agriculture administration & extension.* Vol. 28, No. 2, 1988. pp 101-112

Driel, Antje van (1988), *Bomen groeien niet tot in de hemel. De rurale energie-voorziening in het zuiden van Mali of hoe vrouwen bij de erosiebestrijding kunnen worden betrokken.* Amsterdam: Doctoraal scriptie Sociaal Geografisch Instituut Universiteit van Amsterdam

Dutch Association of University Women, see VVAO

E

Earthwatch, issue (1989), on Women and environment. No. 37, 1989 (4th quarter)   *35*

ECOFORUM, issue (1990), Women and environment. Vol. 14, No. 3, 1990. 16 pp

Ecologist, the; issue (1992), Feminism, nature, development. Vol. 22, No. 1, 1992 (Jan./Feb.)   *35*

Eisenstein, Hester (1984), *Contemporary feminist thought.* London: Unwin. ISBN 0-04301179-9 (UB)

Ekistics, issue (1985), special issue: Women and space in human settlements. No. 310, 1985 (Jan./Feb.) / Backy Dennison Sakelanion (ed.)

El-Hinawi, E., see Martin-Brown, J. and E. El-Hinawi

ELC/Forum '85 (1986), *Women and the environmental crisis,* report of the proceedings of the workshops on Women, Environment and Development, Nairobi 10-20 July 1985, Ed. Dorothy K. Munyakko, ELC (Environment Liaison Centre), Nairobi   *26, 31, 73, 78*

ELCI (1992-1) *Justice between peoples/justice between generations.* Synthesis of Citizens Movements' Responses to Environment and Development Challenges, and *Agenda Ya Wananchi.* Draft Citizens Action Plan for

the 1990's. Prepared for Roots of the Future, a global NGO conference in relation to the 1992. Earth Summit. Paris, 17 to 20 December 1991   *26*
ELCI (1992-2) *Agenda Ya Wananchi.Citizens' Action Plan for the 1990's. Adopted at Roots of the Future, a global NGO conference in relation to the 1992 Earth Summit.* Paris, 17 to 20 December 1991. Nairobi: Environment Liaison Centre International   *26, 28*
Eldredge, H. (et al.) (1990), Gender, science, and technology: a selected annotated bibliography. In: *Behavioral and social sciences librarian.* Vol. 9, No. 1, 1990. pp 77-134 (Inst. 143/UB)   *49*
Elson, Diane (1989), *The impact of structural adjustment on women: concepts and issues.* In: B. Onimode (ed) "The IMF, The World Bank and the African Debt". Vol. II (also in: Royal Tropical Institute, '91 reader)
Emancipatieraad (1990), *Advies: Nationaal milieubeleidsplan en emancipatie.* Den Haag: Emancipatieraad (see also Gilden et al 1990)   *86*
Engo-Tjeda, Ruth Bamela (1991-1), *Attaining African food security while protecting the environment ... did you know?* Paper for the World Women's Congress for a Healthy Planet, Nov. 8-12, 1991 Miami   *66*
Engo-Tjeda, Ruth Bamela (1991-2), *Towards Earth Charter 1992: developing a code of earth ethics integrated with the women's dimension.* Testimony on food security for the World Women's Congress for a Healthy Planet, Nov. 8-12, 1991 Miami   *61*
Environment and Urbanization, issue (1991), Vol. 3, No. 2, 1991 (October) "Women in Environment and Urbanization: Strategies for Action and the Potentials for Change" IIED-America Latina, Argentina (Inst. 162)   *35*
ESMAP/World Bank (1990), Energy Sector Management Assistence Program of World Bank/UNDP/Bilateral Aid, *Women and Energy. The International Network: Policies and Experience.* A resource guide, revised edition September 1990. Washington: ESMAP. Fotocopy available
Evans, Allison (1991), *Socio-economic statistics.* (GMI-Gender Module-IDS) 77p. ISBN 0-9037-1550-3
Evans, Allison (1989), *Gender issues in rural household economics.* (Discussion Paper IDS – D254) 25p. ISBN 0-9037-15-08-2
Evans, A. (1988), *Gender relations and technological change: the need for an integrative framework of analysis.* In: Poats (et al.)(ed). "Gender issues in farming systems research and extension"
Evert Vermeer Stichting (1992), *Op weg van Rio naar Peking. Verslag van een studiedag over Vrouwen, Milieu en Ontwikkeling.* op 31 Oktober 1992. Georganiseerd door de Evert Vermeer Stichting i.s.m. Both Ends, InZet en het Landelijk Milieu Overleg. Amsterdam: EVS

F

FAO/SIDA (1989), *Restoring the balance. Women and forest resources.* Rome: FAO *69*

FAO/Human Resources Institutions & Agrarian Division (1988), *The development of village-based sheep production in West-Africa: a success story involving women's groups.* Training manual for extension workers. Rome: FAO (LEEUW)

FAO, see also Borg, Brigitte v.d./FAO, see also Rojas, Mary/FAO

Faulkner, W & E. Arnold (ed.) (1985), *Smothered by invention: technology in women's lives.* London (etc): Pluto Press. ISBN 0-86104-737-0 (LEEUW)

Feldstein, Hilary Sims and Susan V. Poats (eds.) (1989), *Working together: gender analysis in agriculture.* Vol. 1: case studies. West Harford: Kumarian Press (Kumarian Press case studies series) ISBN 0-931816-58-0 *94*

FEMCONSULT, see Jong-Boon, Carolien de/FEMCONSULT

FEMCONSULT Newsletter, issue (1990), Vol. 1, No. 2, 1990. Special issue on Women, environment and development

Fernandes, Walter & Geeta Menon (1987), *Tribal women and forest economy: deforestation, exploitation and status change.* New Delhi: Indian Social Institute. (Tribes of India Series, 1) (LEEUW) (Inst. 175) (Chapter "Consequences of Deforestation on Forest Dweller Women". pp 84-125 In: reader Schenk-Sandbergen (1991-1) pp 53-74

Food 2000 (1987), *Food 2000: Global policies for sustainable agriculture.* A report of the advisory panel on food security, agriculture, forestry and environment to the World Commission on Environment and Development. London and New Yersey: Zed Books (UB)

Forbes Martin, Susan (1991), *Refugee women.* ZED/UN/NGO group on Women and Development. London: ZED Books. (Women & World Development Series). ISBN 1-85649-001-7

Forum '85, see ELC/Forum '85

Foster, Theodora (1986), *A common future for women and men (and all living creatures).* A Submission to the WCED (World Commission on Environment and Development). Ottawa: EDPRA Consulting Inc. and Associates

Freedom from Debt Coalition, Phillipines, see Briones, Leonor M./Freedom from Debt Coalition

French, Marilyn (1985), *Beyond power: women, men and morality.* New York: Summit Books. ISBN 0-22402-012-9 (UB) *16*

French, David (ed.) (1986), *Agroforestry for food, fuel and income: four project*

approaches focussing on women's work. (Edited and abbridged version of
ILO paper)

Frijns, Jos en Marcel Hazeu (samenstelling/ed.) (1991), *Milieu en Derde
Wereld.* (Reader). Wageningen: Landbouwuniversiteit Wageningen;
Centrum voor Milieustudies   *45, 86*

G

Garibaldi Accati, Elena (1984), Women's role in horticultural production
in developing countries. In: *Science and Public Policy,* Journal of the
Science Policy Foundation. Issue on "Women in Third World
agriculture". Vol. 11, No. 4, 1984 (August) (Inst. 264)

Gender studies in agriculture: a journal of abstracts. Wageningen:
Wageningen Agricultural University; Department of Gender Studies in
Agriculture (Formerly published in Dutch as "Documentatie-bulletin
Vrouwenstudies", 1987-1989) (LUW)   *75*

George, Susan (1992), *The debt boomerang. How Third World debt harms us
all.* London: Pluto Press; TNI ISBN 0-7453-0594-6   *59*

George, Susan (1988), *Debt and the environment: financing ecocide.* In:
Susan George, "A fate worse than debt". pp 115-168   *59*

Ghai, D., see Wolfson, D.J. and D. Ghai

Gilden, A. (et al.) (1990), *Emancipatie en milieu: plussen en minnen op
raakvlakken.* Studie in opdracht van de Emancipatieraad door
Interfacultaire Vakgroep Energie en Milieukunde, Rijksuniversiteit
Groningen. Den Haag: Emancipatieraad (Milieudefensie)   *86*

Gilligan, Carol (1986), *A different voice in moral decisions.* In: Eck, Diana L.
and Devaki Jain (ed), "Speaking of Faith, Cross-Cultural Perspectives
on Women, Religion and Social Change". New Delhi: Committee on
Women, Religion and Social Change, KALI for Women. Fotocopy
available

Gladwin, Christina H. (ed.) (1991), *Structural adjustment and African
women farmers.* Gainesville: University of Florida Press (VENA)

Global Assembly of Women and the Environment "Partners in Life"
(1992-1), *Special report. Findings, recommendations and action plans.*
Washington: Global Assembly Project; WorldWIDE Network. 1992
(January)   *27, 33, 55, 79, 93, 98, 101*

Global Assembly of Women and the Environment "Partners in Life"
(1992-2), *Summary for Prepcom IV. Many mandates for women, follow-up
actions.* Washington: Global Assembly Project; WorldWIDE Network.
1992 (March)   *27, 55, 79, 98*

Global Assembly of Women and the Environment "Partners in Life", held in Miami, USA, 4-8 November 1991. (1991), *Conference map; speeches, participants adresses and success stories.* Washington D.C.: UNEP and WorldWIDE Network   *27, 33, 36, 60, 76, 79, 98*

Goldsmith, E. (1988), The way: an ecological world-view. In: *The Ecologist.* Vol. 18, No. 4/5. pp 160-285 (ISS)   *45, 54*

Goodman, David and Michael Redclift (1991), *Refashioning nature: food, ecology and culture.* London; New York: Routledge. ISBN 0-4506-703-0
46

Governing Council ss III/2, see UNEP/Governing Council ss III/2

Griffin, Susan (1978/1980) *Women and nature; the roaring inside her.* San Francisco: Harper and Row. ISBN 0-06-090744-4   *52*

Grimshaw, Jean (1986), *Feminist philosophers, women's perspectives on philosophical traditions.* Brighton: Wheatsheaf (Inst. 177)

Groen, Bea (1989), *Women and woodfuel; an overview.* In: Netherlands Review of Development Studies/IMWOO. Vol. 2, 1988/89. "Forestry and Development". pp 35-52. ISBN 90-71444-04-X

Groen, Bea C. and Cornie R. Huizenga (1987), *Have planners understood the poor people's energy problem?* Socio-economic aspects of energy technologies: a literature review. Enschede: University of Twente. (Occasional Paper/Technology and Development group Twente University of Technology; No. 4) (ARBOR/KIT)

Groot, Wouter T. de (1992), *Environmental science theory: concepts and methods in a one-world, problem-oriented paradigm.* Amsterdam, etc.: Elsevier Science Publishers B.V. (Studies in Environmental Science; 52) ISBN 0-444-88993-0

Group of green economists, the (1992), *Ecological economics:* a practical programme for global reform. (Preface by Sara Parkin). London: Zed Books. ISBN 1-85649-070-X   *57*

Groverman, Verona (1990), Zorgen om vrouwen en duurzame landbouw. In: *Derde Wereld.* Jrg 9, No. 5, 1991 (Februari). Fotocopy available

Grown, Caren, see Sen, Gita and Caren Grown/DAWN

Grünen im Bundestag, die/AK Frauenpolitik (1987), *Frauen und Oekologie: gegen den Machbarkeitswahn.* Dokumentation zum Kongress vom 3-5 October 1986 in Köln. Beitrage, Berichte, Ausblicke. ISBN 3-923243-29-4
95, 97

Guha, Ramachandra (1991), *The unquiet woods: ecological change and peasant resistance in the Himalaya.* Delhi: Oxford University Press

Guha, Ramachandra (1990), Towards a cross-cultural environmental ethic. In: *Alternatives:* social transformation and human governance. Vol. XV. pp 431-447. Fotocopy available

Gulati, Leela (1984), *Fisherwomen on the Kerala coast: demographic and socio-economic impact of a fisheries development project.* Geneva: ILO (Inst. 189)

Gupta, Jyotsna Agnihotri (1991), Women's bodies: the site for the ongoing conquest by reproductive technologies. In: *Issues in Reproductive and Genetic Engineering.* Vol. 4, No. 2. pp 93-107. Fotocopy available   *62*

Gura, S. (1985), Extension approaches to reach rural women. In: *Training for agriculture and rural development,* 1985. pp 1-89 (LEEUW) (Inst. 189)

H

Habitat, see UNCHS

Haney, Wava G. and Jane B. Knowles (ed.) (1988), *Women and farming: changing roles, changing structures.* Boulder: Westview Press (LEEUW)

Haraway, Donna (1991), *Simians, cyborgs and women: the reinvention of nature.* London: Free Association Books. ISBN 1-85343-139-7   *16, 49*

Haraway, Donna (1989), *Primate visions: gender, race & nature in the world of modern science.* New York/London: Routledge. ISBN 0-415-90114-6   *49*

Harcourt, Wendy (1991-1), *Human centred economics: a gender perspective.* (draft) Paper for the Workshop on Women, the environment and sustainable developnment towards a theoretical framework. The Hague: Institute of Social Studies, 1991 (May, 28)   *40, 41, 58*

Harcourt, Wendy (1991-2), Human security and the gender perspective. In: *Development,* Journal of the Society for International Development. Vol. 1, 1991 "Reflections on Global Solidarity: One World or Several". pp 21-22   *65*

Harding, Sandra (1991), *Whose science? Whose knowledge? Thinking from women's lives.* Ithaca; New York: Cornell University Press (IIAV)   *49*

Harding, Sandra (1986), *The science question in feminism.* Ithaca: Cornell University Press. ISBN 0-8014-1880-1 (Inst. 184/264)   *49*

Hardoy, Jorge E. (et al.) (eds.) (1990), *The poor die young: housing and health in Third World cities.* London: Earthscan ISBN 1-85383-019-4   *70*

Hassan, Farkhonda (ed.) (1989), *Protection of the environment of the river Nile basin: role of women.* (proceedings of the regional symposium Cairo, Egypt, December 1988) / The scientific association of Arab women in Egypt (SAAW)

Hassan, Farkhonda (1988/89), *Biogas technology for rural areas in some Arab countries: implications for women.* American University in Cairo

Hassan, Farkhonda (1986), *Social and cultural aspects of the application of new and renewable energy sources.* American University in Cairo, Egypt ASRE 86, Vol. 2, No. 99. pp 1093-1101. March 23-26 '86

Haugestad, Anne K. (1991), *Immaterial barriers to a sustainable development.* Paper for the Workshop on Women, the environment and sustainable development towards a theoretical framework. The Hague: Institute of Social Studies, 1991 (May, 28)

Haüsler, Sabine and Ewa Charkiewicz-Pluta (1991-1) *Remaking the world together. Women, the environment and sustainable development. A state-of the art-report and a proposal for a reassesment of the topic.* Institute of Social Studies/Department of Women's Studies University of Utrecht, for. INSTRAW (published by ZED Books, London. See Braidotti (et al.)
                                                                           31, 37, 44, 51, 95

Haüsler, Sabine and Ewa Charkiewicz-Pluta (1991-2), *Report on the workshop "Women, the environment and sustainable development towards a theoretical framework",* held at the Institute of Social Studies in The Hague, May 28th 1991

Haverkort, Bertus (et al.)(eds.)/ILEIA (1991-1) *Strenghtening farmers' experiments: a reader with practical experiences and cases of experimenting farmers and how outsiders support them (draft).* Leusden: ILEIA

Haverkort, Bertus (et al.) (eds.)/ILEIA (1991-2), *Joining farmers' experiments: experiences in Participatory Technology Development.* London: Intermediate Technology Publications (ILEIA Readings in Sustainable Agriculture). ISBN 1-85339-101-8   *92*

Hazeu, Marcel, see Frijns, Jos en Marcel Hazeu

Hecht, Susanna and Alexander Cockburn (1989/90), *The fate of the forest: developers, destroyers and defenders of the Amazon.* London etc.: Penguin Books. ISBN 0-14-013382-8   *46*

Hedley, Rachel/IIED (ed.) (1990), *Women, environment, development. Seminar Report,* 7 March 1989. Women's Environmental Network/ War on Want/ OFDA. London: Calvert's Press

Henderson, Hazel (1984), The warp and the weft. The coming synthesis of eco-philosophy and eco-feminism. In: *Development: Seeds of Change,* journal of the Society for International Development. Vol. 4, 1984. In: ISIS International 1991 (information pack)

Hernandez, I., see Veken, M. van der and I. Hernandez

Heyzer, Noeleen (1991), *Gender, economic growth and poverty.* Paper for 20th World Conference of the Society for International Development, Regional Seminar: Women, Economic Development and Poverty. May 6-9 '91, Amsterdam   *24, 39, 40*

Heyzer, Noeleen (ed.) (1987), *Women farmers and rural change in Asia. Towards equal access and participation.* Asian and Pacific Development Centre Kuala Lumpur. ISBN 967-99954-7-X

HIVOS (1989), *Milieu-notitie*. Den Haag: HIVOS   *84, 86*

Hoeksema, Jan (1989), *Women and social forestry. How women can play an active role in programming and implementing forestry projects.* Wageningen: Stichting voor Nederlandse Bosbouw Ontwikkelingssamenwerking. (BOS-Document; No. 10)

Hombergh, Heleen van den/InDRA (1992), *Vrouwen, milieu en ontwikkeling; moet dat nou zo nodig? over een duurzame driehoeksverhouding.* Lezing voor de studiedag over VMO, georganiseerd door Both Ends (et al.) Ook in: BOVO-Nieuwsbrief, April 1992. pp 3-11

Hong, Eveline/Consumers Association of Penang, Malaysia (1985), *Self sufficiency in food related to environmental problems.* (paper for NCO, 24 April 1985)

Hosek, Chaviva (1991), Coming together. In: *Women & Environments.* Vol. 13, No. 2, 1991 (winter/spring). pp 14-17

Hoskins, Marilyn (1979), *Women in forestry for local community development: a programming guide.* Washington: USAID Office of Women in Development. Also in Lewis, Barbara 1981. (VENA)

Hoven van den, Laurien (1990), *The feminin principle, a study of the attitude towards trees in a village in Tamil Nadu, India.* Thesis M.A. in Anthropology. Anthropological Sociological Centre, University of Amsterdam (Inst. 175)   *31*

Hueting, R. (et al.) (1992), *Methodology for the calculation of sustainable national income.* Statistische Onderzoekingen (M-reeks). 's-Gravenhage: SDU uitgeverij/CBS-Publikaties. (Centraal Bureau voor de Statistiek, Statistische onderzoekingen, M44). ISBN 90-3571-370-2 (Inst. 310)   *57*

Human Resources, Institutions & Agrarian Division, see FAO/Human Resources, Institutions & Agrarian Division

Huijsman, Marijk (1991), *Leven van afval, een onderzoek naar de gender aspekten van het vuilrapen in de Zuid-Indiase stad Bangalore, India.* Skriptie voor ASC

Huizinga, Cornie R., see Groen, Bea C. and Cornie R. Huizinga

Hynes, H. Patricia (1989-1) *The recurring silent spring.* New York etc.: Pergamon Press. (The Athene Series) ISBN 0-08-037116-7   *63, 64*

Hynes, H. Patricia (ed.) (1989-2) *Reconstructing Babylon: women and technology.* London: Earthscan Publications Ltd. ISBN 1-85383-057-7 *63, 64*

Hypatia: a journal of feminist philosophy, special issue (1991), Ecological Feminism / edited by Karen J. Warren. Vol. 6, No. 1, 1991 (Spring) ISSN 0887-5367

I

ICIMOD (1989), *Women in mountain development,* report of the international workshop on Women, Development, and Mountain Resources: approaches to Internalising Gender Perspectives. Organised by ICIMOD (the International Centre for Integrated Mountain Development), Kathmandhu, Nepal 21-24 November 1988, ICIMOD Nepal. Fotocopy available

ICRW (1991), *Project report on "Women, poverty and environment in Latin America".* Washington: International Centre for Research on Women

IDOC Internationale, issue (1989), "When sister earth suffers, women suffer too". Vol. 19, No. 3, 1989 (May-June). Rome, Italy. ISSN 0250-76431

Idris, S.M. Mohamed (1991), *Being "green" from the Third World Viewpoint.* In: Frijns & Hazeu (1991)

IIED, see Hedley, Rachel/IIED

ILEIA (bibliography) (1988), *Towards sustainable agriculture,* part 2, ILEIA/Agrecol, Leusden, the Netherlands, May 1988

ILEIA, see also Haverkort, Bertus (et al.)/ILEA

ILO (1988), *Women and land.* Report on the regional African workshop on women's access to land as a strategy for employment promotion, poverty alleviation and household food security, organized by the Intenational Labour Office in collaboration with the University of Zimbabwe, in Harare, Zimbabwe, from 17-21 October 1988. Geneva: ILO

74

ILO (1987), *The rural energy crisis, women's work and basic needs.* Proceedings of International Workshop co-sponsored by the ILO and the ISS, The Hague, 21-24 April 1986. Geneva: ILO. ISBN 92-2-105802-6. Fotocopy available

ILO (1986), *Energy and rural women's work.* Vol. II. Papers of a prepatory meeting on energy and rural women's work, Geneva 21-25 October 1985. Geneva: ILO (Both Ends) (VENA)

ILO (1985), *Resources, power and women.* Proceedings of the African & Asian Inter-regional workshops on strategies for improving the employment conditions of rural women, Arusha, United Republic of Tanzania 20-25 August 1984. Geneva: ILO. ISBN 92-2-105009-2

ILO, see also Cecelski, Elisabeth/ILO

InDRA (1993), *People, Environment and Development: the urgent need for transformation.* Thematic reader for the lecture series 1992/1993. Amsterdam: Institute for Development Research Amsterdam

InDRA (1991/1-2), *Boundaries and identities; heritages of colonial past and current ethnic relations.* Reader interfacultary lecture series Development

Studies '91-'92, part 1: general reader, part 2: thematic reader. Compiled by Margriet Poppema and Pyt Douma. Amsterdam: University of Amsterdam, InDRA

InDRA, see also Hombergh, Heleen van den/InDRA, see also Wieberdink, Ange/InDRA

Inglis, A.S. (1988), *Rural women and urban men: fuelwood conflicts and forest sustainability in Sussex Village, Sierra Leone*. London: ODI (Social forestry network paper 6) (ARBOR)

INSTRAW (1992), *Policy development resource portfolio on gender, environment and sustainable development*. Santo Domingo, Dominican Republic:. INSTRAW

INSTRAW (1989), *Women, water supply and sanitation, making the link stronger*. Santo Domingo, Dominican Republic:. INSTRAW   70

INSTRAW (1988), *UN and non-UN sources dealing with women and NRSE* (New and Renewable Sources of Energy). Annotated bibliography (1980-1987), 73 titles. ILO/INSTRAW

INSTRAW (1985-1), *Women & technology in developing countries: technological change and women's capabilities and bargaining position*. Santo Domingo, Dominican Republic: UN/INSTRAW

INSTRAW (1985-2), *Toward strategies for strengthening the position of women in food production: an overview and proposals on Africa*. Santo Domingo, Dominican Republic: UN/INSTRAW

INSTRAW (1985-3), *Summary of INSTRAW series of studies on the role of women in international economic relations*. Santo Domingo, Dominican Republic:. INSTRAW

INSTRAW News, issue (1988), New and renewable sources of energy, an option for women, a challenge to the future (Women and Development) No. 10 spring/summer '88

International Women's Tribune Centre, see IWTC, see also Sandhu, Ruby and Joanne Sandler/International Women's Tribune Centre

ISIS International (1991), *Women's action for the environment. Information pack*. Quezon City, Phillipines: ISIS Recource Center and Information program   35

ISIS International (1990), *Directory of Third World women's publications*. Quezon City (The Philippines): ISIS International

ISS, see Lycklama a Nijeholt (ed.)

IUCN (et al.) (1991), *Caring for the earth. A strategy for sustainable development*. (Senior consultant and writer: Robert Prescott-Allen/final text ed. by David A. Munro and Martin W. Holdgate) Gland: IUCN,

The World Conservation Union; United Nations Environment
Programme; World Wide Fund for Nature. ISBN 2-8317-0074-4   *26, 78*
IUCN (1988), Report workshop *Women and the IUCN programme,* IUCN 17th
General Assembly 1988 (Both Ends)   *77*
IUCN (1987-1), *IUCN Conference Women and the World Conservation Strategy,*
November 25-27 1987, Gland Switzerland. Conference map, including
papers and draft recommandations   *77*
IUCN (1987-2) *Women and the World Conservation Strategy:* report on the
first strategy workshop "Population and sustainable development
programme". Fotocopy available   *77*
IUCN (et al.) (1980), *The World Conservation Strategy.* Geneva: IUCN, UNEP,
WWF   *25, 77*
IWTC (1990), *Women and water: a collection of IWTC newsletters on issues,*
activities and resources in the area of women, water and sanitation needs.
New York: International Women's Tribune Center (VENA)
IYSH (1987), *Women and shelter seminar,* November-December 1987,
Harare, Zimbabwe. Seminar report   *99*

J

Jacobson, Jodi L. (1992), Gender bias: roadblock to sustainable
development. In: *Worldwatch Paper,* No. 110. September 1992. pp 1-60
(also in: InDRA Reader 1993)
Jain, Devaki (1991), Can we have a women's agenda for global
development? In: *Development,* journal of the Society for International
Development. Vol. 1, 1991 "Reflections on Global Solidarity: One world
or Several". pp 74-78   *55*
Jansen, Mirjam (comp.) (1990), *Ecofeminisme,* (bibliografie over
ecofeminisme i.r.t. spiritualiteit/ religie/ andogynie/ antropologie/
psychoanalyse/ socialisatie/ militarisme/ landbouw
(-wetenschappen)/feministische wetenschappen/ gender-milieu
onderzoek/ groene vrouwenbeweging). Nijmegen: Derde Wereld
Centrum   *49*
Joekes, Susan (1989), *Population growth, sustainable development and the role*
of women (paper) for the World Bank, Women in Development
Division, Population and Human Resources Department   *62, 81*
Joekes, Susan, see also Kabeer, Naila and Susan Joekes (eds.)
Johns, D.M. (1990), The relevance of deep ecology to the Third World:
some preliminary comments. In: *Environmental Ethics.* Vol. 12, 1990
(fall) pp 233-253   *52*
Jommo, Rosemary Berewa (1992), *Technology and scientific research in*

relation to indigenous knowledge. Speech for InDRA's lecture series, Feb. 13th, Amsterdam   *74*

Jong-Boon, Carolien de/FEMCONSULT (1992), *Women, environment and development in UNCED. Discussion paper for the preparations of UNCED, in particular PrepCom IV.* Paper prepared at the request of the Special Programme on Women and Development, DGIS, Ministry of Development Coöperation, The Netherlands   *79*

Jong-Boon, Caroline de (ed.) (1990), *Environmental problems in the Sudan: a reader. Part I and II.* The Hague: Institute of Social Studies (ISS/DGIS)

Journal of Rural Studies, issue (1991), "Women in agriculture". Vol. 7, No. 1/2, 1991. Oxford etc: Pergamon Press (Inst. 162)

JUNIC/NGO (1988-1), *The key to development: women's social and economic role, kit No. 3* Joint United Nations Information Committee NGO's subgroup on women and development

JUNIC/NGO (bibliography) (1988-2), Women and the world economic crisis. Part V: Resource guide. In: *JUNIC/ NGO women's kit No. 6*   *59*

JUNIC/NGO (1988-3), *Women and peace, equality, participation, development. Kit No. 5.* Issued at the Unit. Nations Office at Vienna (UNOV) by the Division for the Advancement of women

K

Kabeer, Naila (1991-1), Gender dimensions of rural poverty. Analysis from Bangladesh. In: *The Journal of Peasant Studies.* Vol. 18, No. 2. 1991 (January). pp 241-262 (Inst. 162/175)

Kabeer, Naila and Susan Joekes (eds.) (1991-2) *Researching the household: methodological and empirical issues.* (IDS Bulletin, Vol. 22, No. 1 (January 1991)

Kabeer, Naila (1989), *Women: agriculture and rural problems: monitoring poverty as if gender mattered. Methodology for Bangladesh.* (IDS discussion papers; D255 Sussex.)(KIT). Also in: Royal Tropical Institute 1990; reader. pp 192-216

Kalb, M., see Monson, J. and M. Kalb

Kalpagan, U. (1985), Coping with urban poverty in India. In: *Bulletin of Concerned Asian scholars.* pp 2-18. In: reader Schenk-Sandbergen (1991-II) pp 257-273

Kelkar, Govind and Dev Nathan (1991), *Gender and tribe. Women, land and the forests.* London: ZED Books

Keller, Evelyn Fox (1985), *Reflections on gender and science.* New Haven: Yale University Press. (UB)   *49*

Kessler, S (1985), *Third World women in agriculture: an annotated bibliography.* New York (etc): National Council for Research on women (LEEUW)

Khasiani, Shanyisa A. (ed.) (1992), *Groundwork. African women as environmental managers.* Nairobi: African Center for Technology Studies Press

Khor Kok, Martin, see Raman, Meenakshi

King, Deirdie (1989), *Rural women and environmental sustainability. The impact of the fuelwood and water crises on rural women.* (Msc. essay), University of Bradford, West Yorkshire. (VENA)

King, Ynestra (1990), *Healing the wounds; feminism, ecology, and the nature/ culture dualism.* In: Diamond and Orenstein, "Reweaving the world: ...". pp 106-121 (Same title appeared earlier in: Alison M. Jaggar and Susan R. Bordo (ed) 'Gender, body, knowledge.' Rutgers, The State of University. pp 115-141   *50, 52*

King, Ynestra (1989), *The ecology of feminism and the feminism of ecology.* In: Judith Plant "Healing the wounds". pp 18-28. Same title appeared earlier in: Communities: journal of cooperative living, 1988, 75, Summer pp 32-38   *16, 47, 51*

King, Ynestra (1987), What is eco-feminism. In: *The Nation.* 1987 (12 December)

King, Ynestra (1983-1) *Feminism and the revolt of nature.* Women's International Network, Lexington, USA. In: ISIS International 1991 (information pack)   *50*

King, Ynestra (1983-2), *The eco-feminist imperative.* In: Caldecott et al (ed) '83 op. cit

Kinnaird, Viviam, see Momsen, Janet and Viviam Kinnaird

Kishwar, Madhu and Ruth Vanita (ed.) (1984), *In search of answers. Indian women's voices from "Manushi".* London: Zed Books (Third World Studies) ISBN 0-86232-178-6   *96*

KIT, see Royal Tropical Institute

Kjellberg Bell, Judith (1991), Women, environment and urbanization: a guide to the literature. In: *Environment and Urbanization.* Vol. 3, No. 2, 1991 (October) pp 92-103. Fotocopy available   *99*

Knowles, Jane B., see Haney, Wava G. and Jane B. Knowles

Kreiman, Adriana (1985), Influencia que la mujer puede ejercer para asegurar una adecuada proteccion ambiental. In: *Ambiente y recursos naturales, revista de derecho, politica y administracion.* Publicacion trimestral de la Fundacion ARN, Buenos Aires, Argentina. Vol. II, No. 4, 1985 (Oct.-Dic.) pp 14-19

Kumar-D'Souza, Corinne (1991), *The South wind.* Paper for 20th World

Conference of the Society for International Development. Women, peace and development plenary, 6-9th May 1991, Amsterdam   *43, 51*

L
Lappé, Frances Moore and Joseph Collins (1986/1988), *World hunger: twelve myths.* London: Earthscan Publications Ltd. ISBN 1-85383-012-7
62, 66
Lappé, Frances Moore and Rachel Schurman (1988/1989), *Taking population seriously.* London: Earthscan Publications Ltd. ISBN 1-85383-055-0
Leach, Gerald and Robin Mearns (1988), *Beyond the woodfuel crisis. People, land and trees in Africa.* London: Earthscan (reviewed in IDS public. 1991) ISBN 1-85383-031-3 (Inst. 162)
Leach, Gerald (1987), Energy and the Urban poor. In: *IDS Bulletin.* Vol. 18, No. 1, 1987. pp 31-38. In: reader Schenk-Sandbergen (1991-1) pp 149-156
Leach, Melissa (1991-1) *Gender and the environment: traps and opportunities.* Paper prepared for Development Studies Association (DSA) Conference, Swansea, September 11-13 '91. Brighton: Institute of Development Studies, University of Sussex   *50, 51, 94*
Leach, Melissa and Robin Mearns (1991-2) *Environmental change, development challenges.* (IDS Bulletin, Vol. 22, No. 4 (October 1991)
Leach, Melissa, see also Davies, S and Melissa Leach (eds.)
Leacock, Eleanor and Helen I. Safa (eds.) (1986), *Women's work, development and the division of labour by gender.* South Hadley, Mass: Bergin & Gawey. ISBN 0-89789-035-3 (Inst. 174)
Leeuwen, Nan van (1990), *Farm-household systems and gender impact analysis: a framework for target group analysis and gender issues,* paper for Third course on the design of Community Forestry, October 1-5 1990 at the International agricultural Centre, Wageningen
Letsch, Mirjam (1993), *Will the twain ever meet?* Towards a contextual understanding of community participation processes under the Indo-Dutch Project in the stratified society of Mirzapur City, Uttar Pradesh (India). Amsterdam: Antropologisch-Sociologisch Centrum; University of Amsterdam   *70*
Letsch, Mirjam (1990), *Community participation for water supply and sanitary facilities in low-income urban areas in Asia.* A discussion on the "hard reality" of the "soft side". The Hague: International Reference Centre for Water and Sanitation. (IRC)
Levy, Caren (1992), Gender and the environment: the challenge of

cross-cutting issues in development policy and planning. In:
Environment and Urbanization. Vol. 4, No. 1, April 1992. pp 134-150
                                                           75, 82, 90, 92
Lewis, Barbara (1981), *Invisible farmers: women and the crisis in agriculture.*
Washington: WID/AID, AID/OTR-C-147-35
Ling, Chee Yoke (1989), Women, environment and development; the
Malaysian experience. In: *Development,* journal of the Society for
International Development. Vol. 2/3, 1989. pp 88-91. Also in: Wallace,
T. and Candida March: Changing Perceptions. Writings on Gender
and Development. pp 22-29 "The impact of global crises on women" *70*
Linggard, Trine; Mette Moberg (1990), *Women and sustainable
development: a report from Women's Forum in Bergen, Norway 14-15 May
1990.* Oslo: Center for Information on Women and Development
                                                           19, 32, 58, 86
Litvinoff, Miles, see Conroy, Czech and Miles Litvinoff
Loudiyi, Dounia (1991), *Women and natural resources management, an
annotated bibliography.* IUCN, Social Sciences Division. Washington DC:
IUCN-US (draft)
Loudiyi, Dounia (et al.) (1988), *The African Women's Assembly: women and
sustainable development.* Washington DC: IUCN/WRI/Worldwide *33, 79, 85*
Lycklama à Nijeholt, Geertje (ed.)/ISS (1991), *Towards women's strategies for
the 1990's: challenging government and the state.* London: Macmillan
Academic and Professional Ltd. ISBN 0-333-56061-2
Lycklama à Nijeholt, Geertje (1987), *The fallacy of integration: the UN
strategy of integrating women revisited.* In: Netherlands Review of
Development Studies. Vol. 1, 1987. Also in: Reader Royal Tropical
Institute, 1991   *40*

M

Maathai, Wangari (1991), *People's rights, participation and resources: decisions
and actions for sustainable development with justice and equity.* Speech for
World Women's Conference for A Healthy Planet, Miami, Nov. 8-12,
1991
Maathai, Wangari (1988), *The Green Belt Movement. Sharing the approach
and the experience.* Nairobi: ELCI   *98*
Maathai, Wangari (1984), *The Green Belt Movement.* Nairobi: General
Printers Ltd   *98*
MacCormack, Carol and Marilyn Strathern (ed.) (1980), *Nature, culture
and gender.* Cambridge: Cambridge University Press. ISBN 0-52123-491-3
(Inst. 176/315)

Malnes, Raino (1990), *The environment and duties to future generations: an elaboration of sustainable development*. Report 1990/2, Research Programme "Energy, environment and development", ECON/FNI, Oslo and Lysaker, Norway '90. Fotocopy available

Mamdani, Mahmood (1981), *The ideology of population control*. In: K.L. Michaelson (ed) "And the poor get children. Radical Perspectives on Population Dynamics". In: reader Schenk-Sandbergen (1991-II), pp 436-442

March, Candida, see Wallace, Tina and Candida March

March & Taggu (1986), *Informal associations: defensive or active*. In: March & Taggu "Women's informal associations in Developing Countries". Boulder; London: Westview Press. Chapter 3, p II   *99*

Martin-Brown, J. and E. El-Hinnawi (1988), *Women and the environment*. Doc 0667v (y. Mirza) (dealt with in Loudiyi). Fotocopy available   *71, 89*

Mbilini, Marjorie (1991), *Beyond oppression and crisis: a gendered analysis of agrarian structure and change*. Paper prepared for CODESRIA Workshop on Gender Analysis and African Social Science, Dakar, September, 16-21, 1991 (on Tanzania)

McCracken, J.A. (et al.) (1988), *An introduction to Rapid Rural Appraisal for agricultural development*. IIED (LUW)

Meadows, D. (et al.) (1972), *The limits to growth*. New York: Universe Books. (A Potomac Associates Book). ISBN 0-87663-165-0   *25*

Mearns, Robin, see Leach, Gerald and Robin Mearns, see Leach, Melissa and Robin Mearns

Menon, Geeta, see Fernandes, Walter and Geeta Menon

Merchant, Carolyn (1992), *Radical ecology: the search for a livable world*. New York; London: Routledge. ISBN 0-415-90650-4   *48*

Merchant, Carolyn (1980/1983/1989), *The death of nature: women, ecology and the scientific revolution*. New York: Harper Collins Publishers, 1989. ISBN 0-06-250595-5   *48, 96*

Mies, Maria and Vandana Shiva (1993), *Ecofeminism*. London: ZED Books. ISBN 1-85649-156-0   *49*

Mies, Maria (1991), *Consumption patterns of the North – the cause of environmental destruction and poverty in the South, "Women and Children First"*. UNCED/UNICEF/UNFPA Symposium Geneva, 27-30 May 1991. Research paper No. 21   *61*

Mies, Maria (1988), *Social origins of the sexual division of labour*. In: Maria Mies, Veronika Bennholdt-Thomsen and Claudia von Werlhof, "Women: the last colony", part 2: Colonization of women and nature. London and New Jersey: Zed Books (VENA)   *49*

Mies, Maria (1986), *Patriarchy and accumulation on a world scale: women in the international division of labour.* London: Zed Press. ISBN 0-86232-342-8

Mies, Maria, see also Salleh, Ariel & Maria Mies

Milbrath, Lester W. (1989), *Envisioning a sustainable society; learning our way out.* New York: State University of New York Press. (SUNY Series in Environmental Public Policy) ISBN 0-7914-0163-4

Ministerie v. Sociale Zaken & Werkgelegenheid (1990), *Werkboek over de toekomstgerichte strategieen v.d. Verenigde Naties voor de verbetering v.d. positie van vrouwen.* ('85 – 2000) (SZW, Delft) (Both Ends) (VENA)

Ministry of Foreign Affairs Netherlands/DGIS (1992), *Explanatory notes on "Development Screening" of project assistance.* Internal document   *84, 90*

Ministry of Foreign affairs, Netherlands/DGIS (1991-1), *Vrouwen en ontwikkeling, een literatuurlijst (Women and development, a literature list).* Den Haag: Dienst Documentaire Informatievoorziening

Ministry of Foreign affairs, Netherlands/DGIS (1991-2), *Milieu en ontwikkeling, een literatuurlijst (Environment and development, a literature list).* Den Haag: Dienst Documentaire Informatievoorziening

Ministry of Foreign Affairs, Netherlands/ DGIS (1990), *Women, energy, forestry and environment. Policy on an operational footing: main points and checklists.* The Hague: DGIS (Sector Paper Women and Development; No. 4)   *84, 90, 104*

Ministry of Foreign Affairs, Netherlands /DGIS (1989-1), *Women and agriculture. Policy on an operational footing: main points and checklists.* The Hague: DGIS (Sector papaer women and development; No. 1)   *84*

Ministry of Foreign Affairs Netherlands /DGIS (1989-2), *Women, water and sanitation. Policy on an operational footing: main points and checklists.* The Hague: DGIS (Sector paper women and development; No. 2)   *84*

Ministry of Foreign Affairs, Netherlands /DGIS (1989-3), *Women and health. Policy on an operational footing: main points and checklists.* The Hague; DGIS (Sector paper women and development; No. 3)   *84*

Ministry of Foreign Affairs, Netherlands/DGIS (1987), *Women and development. Programme of action.* The Hague: DGIS   *84*

Ministry of Housing, Physical Planning and Environment, see VROM

Mitlin, Diana (1992), Sustainable development: a guide to literature. In: *Environment and Urbanization.* Vol. 4, No. 1, 1992 (April)   *44, 45, 54, 78*

Moberg, Mette, see Linggard, Trine; Mette Moberg

Mobers, Maria (1988), *Agrarische vrouwen en milieu, werkmap.* Amsterdam: Vereniging Milieudefensie/Milieukompas (Milieudefensie)

Molnar, Augusta and Goetz Schreiber (1989), *Women and forestry:*

operational issues. Washington: The World Bank. (Policy, Planning and Research Working Papers-Women in Development; WPS 184). Fotocopy available (VENA)

Molnar, Augusta (1987), *Forest conservation in Nepal: encouraging women's participation,* seeds (pamphlet); No. 10, New York. ISSN 073-6833. Fotocopy available

Molnar, Augusta, see also Stone, Andrew and Augusta Molnar

Molyneux, Maxine (1987), *Mobilization without emancipation? Women's interests, state and revolution in Nicaragua.* Slater, D. (ed), New Social Movements and the State in Latin America. (also in: reader Royal Tropical Institute 1991)   53

Momsen, Janet and Viviam Kinnaird (1993), *Different places, different voices: gender and development in Africa, Asia and Latin America.* London: Routledge (IIAV)

Momsen, J.H. and J. G. Townsend (ed.) (1987), *Geography of gender in the Third World.* Hutchinson: State University of New York Press

Monimart, Marie (1989-1), *Women in the fight against desertification.* CILSS and Club du Sahel, Ouagadougou Burkina Faso (also IIED paper, No. 12)

Monimart, Marie et M. Brah (1989-2), *Femmes du Sahel: la désertification au quotidien.* Paris: Editions Karthala/OCDE/Club du Sahel. ISBN 2-86537-237-5

Monson, J & M. Kalb (ed.) (1985), *Women as food producers in developing countries.* Los Angeles (etc): University of California (etc.) (LEEUW)

Moser, Caroline (et al.) (1991), *The urban context: women, settlements and the environment.* In: Sally Sontheimer (ed), "Women and the environment, a reader: crisis and development in the Third World"

Moser, Caroline O.N. (1989-1), Gender planning in the Third World: meeting practical and strategic gender needs. In: *World Development.* Vol. 17, No. 11, 1989. pp 1799-1825. Also in: Reader Royal Tropical Institute, 1991. Also available in Spanish   *16, 24, 39, 40, 53, 87, 88*

Moser, Caroline (1989-2), *Community participation in urban projects in the Third World.* Oxford etc.: Pergamon. (Progress in planning, 32; 2) (UB)

Moser, Caroline O.N. (1987-1) *Mobilization is women's work: struggles for infrastructure in Guayaquil, Ecuador.* In: Moser and Peake (eds) 1987, pp 166-194. Fotocopy available

Moser, Caroline O.N. & Linda Peake (eds.) (1987-2), *Women, human settlements & housing.* London: Tavistock. ISBN 0-42261-860-8 (Inst. 164/166)

Moser, Caroline O.N. and Caren Levy (1986), *A theory and methodology of gender planning: meeting women's practical and strategic needs.* London: Univ. College London, Barlett School of Architecture and Planning, Development Planning Unit. (DPU Gender and Planning Working paper; No. 11) (Inst. 174)   *40, 87*

Muller, Maria S. and Dorine Plantenga (1990), *Women and habitat: urban management, empowerment and women's strategies.* Amsterdam: Royal Tropical Institute Amsterdam. (Royal Tropical Institute, Bulletin, 321) (Inst. 323)   *98*

Muller, Maria S. en Dorine Plantenga (red.) (1987), *De Volkswijk, woning en werkplaats: overlevingsstrategieën van vrouwen in Derde-Wereldsteden.* Amsterdam: Koninklijk Instituut voor de Tropen. ISBN 90-6832-020-3 *98*

Muller, Maria S., see also Plantenga, Dorine and Maria S. Muller

Muntemba, Shimwaayi (1985-1), *Vrouwen, de boeren van Afrika.* In: "Geen oplossingen zonder vrouwen, verslag Vrouwen en plattelandsontwikkeling", NCO platform, 1985. pp 9-14

Muntemba, Shimwaayi (1985-2), *Rural development and women: lessons from the field.* Vol. 1: Women in production and marketing and their access to credit. Geneva: ILO. ISBN 92-2-105152-8

Murphy, Yolanda & R.F. Murphy (1985), *Women of the forest. Second edition.* New York etc.: Columbia University Press. ISBN 0-231-06089-0 (ISS) (Inst. 176)

Mwalo, Margaret (1991), *Population and gender issues in social sciences.* Paper prepared for the CODESRIA Workshop on Gender Analysis and Social Sciences. Dakar, September, 16-21, 1991

N

Nadel, J.H., see Davis, D.L. and J.H. Nadel (eds.)

Naess, A. (1989/1990), *Ecology, community and life style.* Outline of an ecosophy. Cambridge: Cambridge University Press. ISBN 0-521-34406-9 (Inst. 126)   *47*

NAR (1992), *Nader advies UNCED,* in aanvulling op het briefadvies van 16 December 1991, 16 Februari 1992. Den Haag: Nationale Adviesraad voor Ontwikkelingssamenwerking

NAR (1991), *Briefadvies UNCED 16 December 1991.* Den Haag: Nationale Adviesraad voor Ontwikkelingssamenwerking

Narain, Sunita, see Agarwal, Anil and Sunita Narain

Nathan, Dev (1990), Women and forests. In: *Economic and Political weekly.* 1990 (April 14) pp 795-797 (also in reader Sprenger '91)   *31*

Nathan, Dev, see also Kelkar, Govind and Dev Nathan

Natiyal, K., see Sharma K.B. Pandey and K. Natiyal

Nederlandse Vrouwen Raad (1990), *Bevolkingspolitiek.* Den Haag: NVR. (INFO Reeks; No. 32, December 1990)

Neerbos, Ria van (samenst.)/VeSO (1992), *Vrouwen en de schuldencrisis; een geannoteerde bibliografie.* Amsterdam: Vrouwen en Schulden Overleg. ISBN 90-800859-1-X   *59*

NGLS (1987), *Case studies from Africa: towards food security.* Advocates for African food security lessening the burden for women. New York: United Nations

Nichols, R., see Abramovitz, Janet N. and R. Nichols

Noord-Zuid Campagne (1988), *Vrouwen en de schuldencrisis,* 8 maart, internationale vrouwendag, conferentiemap, Cultureel- en Congrescentrum de Reehorst, Ede. Noord-Zuid Campagne 1988

Noske, Barbara (1990), *Staat dier tot mens als vrouw tot man?* In: Raymond Corbey en Paul v.d. Grijp (red.) "Natuur en Cultuur, beschouwingen op het raakvlak van antropologie en filosofie". pp 75-85 (Book available at InDRA)

Noske, Barbara (1988), *Huilen met de wolven: een interdisciplinaire benadering van de mens-dier relatie.* Amsterdam: Van Gennep. Proefschrift Universiteit van Amsterdam. (Inst. 176/242)

O

Obel, E. (1989), Women and afforestation in Kenya. In: *Voices from Africa.* No. 1, 1989. pp 15-26

Ochs, Kathleen H., see Bicocci, Cynthia Gay & Kathleen H. Ochs

OECD, see DAC/OECD

Oever, Pietronella van den (1991), *Women's roles, population issues, poverty and environmental degradation.* "Women and Children First." UNCED/UNICEF/UNFPA Symposium Geneva, 27-30 May 1991. Research paper No. 15   *61, 77*

Ofosu-Amaah, Waafas and L.A. Shotwell/WorldWIDE Network (1991), *The Latin American and the Carribean Regional Assembly: Women and the Environment, Quito, Ecuador, March 19-22 1991* (report based on the approved document of the plenary session of this Regional Assembly)
33, 79

Omvedt, Gail (1992), Ecofeminism in action: healing India with women's power. In: *Guardian; Independent Radical Newsweekly.* March 25, 1992. pp 10-11. Fotocopy available   *96, 97*

Orenstein, Gloria F., see Diamond, Irene and Gloria F. Orenstein

Outshoorn, Joyce (1989), *Een irriterend onderwerp. Verschuivende conceptualiseringen van het sekseverschil.* Rede uitgesproken bij de

aanvaarding van het ambt van gewoon hoogleraar in de vrouwenstudies
aan de Rijksuniversiteit te Leiden op dinsdag 31 Januari 1989. Nijmegen:
SUN   28

Overholt, C. (et al.) (eds.) (1985), *Gender roles in development projects: a
casebook.* West Hartford, Connecticut: Kumarian Press. ISBN
0-931816-15-7   88

P

Palmer, I. (1988/1990), *Gender issues in structural adjustment of Sub-Saharan
African agriculture and some demographic implications.* Working paper/
World Employment Programme Research 2-21, Working paper/
Population and policies programme No. 166, International Labour
Office Geneva, Switserland 1990. 2nd impr. (Inst. 189) (LEEUW)

Palmer, Ingrid (1985), *The impact of male-out migration on women in
farming.* West Hartford: Kumarian Press. (Serie Women's Roles &
Gender Differences in Development. Cases for Planners)

Pandey, S. (1985), *Nepalese women in natural resource management.* In:
"Training for Agriculture and rural development". FAO/Unesco/ILO
(LEEUW)

Parpart, J.L., see Stichter, S.B. and J.L. Parpart

Peake, Linda, see Moser, Caroline O.N. and Linda Peake

Pearson, R. (1988), *Female workers in the First and Third Worlds: the
greening of women's labour.* In: Pahl, R.E. (ed) "On work: historical,
comparative and theoretical approaches". Oxford (etc): Blackwell. pp
463-466 (UB/Inst. 157)

People's Health Network, see Ramprasad, Vanaja/People's Health Network

Pietilä, Hilkka and Jeanne Vickers (1990), *Making women matter: the role of
the United Nations.* London: Zed books. ISBN 0-86232-969-8   86

Pietilä, Hilkka (1985), *Tomorrow begins today. Alternative development with
women in the North.* ICDA/ISIS Workshop in Forum '85 Nairobi 10/19-7
'85

Pintasilgo, Dr. Maria de Lourdes Pintasilgo (1987), *New energy needed:
women's leadership.* Lezing Bernardijn ter Zeldam Stichting, Amsterdam

Plant, Judith (ed) (1989), *Healing the wounds: the promise of ecofeminism.*
Philadelphia: New Society Publishers. ISBN 1-85425-016-7   51

Plantenga, Dorine, see Muller, Maria S. en Dorine Plantenga (1990 en
1987)

Plas, Barbara van der (1992), *"Vrouwen Actie Agenda 21": een brochure over
vrouwen, milieu en ontwikkeling.* Amsterdam; Oegstgeest: Both Ends;
Vrouwenberaad Ontwikkelingssamenwerking; WEMOS

Plumwood, Val (1992), Feminism and ecofeminism: beyond the dualistic assumptions of women, men and nature. In: *The Ecologist.* Vol. 22, No. 1, 1992 (Jan./Feb.) (Also in: InDRA Reader 1993)   *51*

Plumwood, Val (1991), Natural, self and gender: feminism, enviromental philosophy and the critique of rationalism. In: *Hypatia: a journal of Feminist Philosophy.* Vol. 6, No. 1, 1991 (Spring) pp 3-27. (this number of the journal available at InDRA)

Plumwood, Val (1988), Women, humanity and nature. In: *Radical Philosophy.* No. 48, 1988 (spring) pp 16-24

Poats, S.V. (et al.) (1989), *Gender and intra/inter-household analysis in on-farm research and experimentation.* In: Wilk R.R. (ed) "The household economy: reconsidering the domestic mode of production". Boulder: Westview Press. pp 245-266 (LEEUW)   *88*

Poats, Susan V. (et al.) (eds.) (1988), *Gender issues in Farming Systems Research and Extension.* Boulder and London: Westview Press. (Westview Special Studies in Agriculture Science and Policy) ISBN 0-8133-7399-9   *75, 88, 90, 92, 94*

Poats, Susan V., see also Feldstein, Hillary Sims and Susan V. Poats

Pollard, Robert (et al.) (1992), *Alternative treaties. Synergistic processes for sustainable communities and global responsibility.* A revised edition of the Alternative Treaties from the International NGO Forum, Rio de Janeiro, June 1-14, 1992. Bedfordshire: Ideas for Tomorrow Today and International Synergy Institute   *26, 28, 35, 61, 62, 103*

Postel, Els (1990), *Participation in practice: conservation strategies with women.* In: M. Marchand and H.A. Udo de Haes (ed.) "The people's role in wetland management, proceedings of the International Conference on Wetlands. The Netherlands, Leiden 5-8 June 1989". pp 75-82. Fotocopy available   *40*

Postel, E. en M. Boesveld (1989-1), Milieubeleid en planning met vrouwen: onderzoek en praktijk. In: *IMWOO bulletin.* Vol. 17, No. 3, 1989. pp 17-19

Postel-Coster, Els (1989-2), De paradox van bevolkingsbeleid. In: *Derde Wereld.* Jrg. 8. No. 3, 1989 (October) pp 70-76

Prah, K.K. (1991), *Sex and access: selected gender issues in the livestock, fisheries and wildlife sectors in Eastern and Southern Africa.* Paper prepared for CODESRIA Workshop on Gender Analysis and African Social Science, Dakar, September, 16-21, 1991   *75*

Prentice, Susan (1988), Taking sides: what's wrong with ecofeminism?. In: *Women and Environments.* Vol. 10, No. 3, 1988. pp 9-10 Also in: Sprenger '91, and ISIS International 1991 (information pack)   *51*

PrepCom II, see UNCED/Filomina Chioma Steady/PrepCom II

PrepCom III, see UNCED/Filomina Chioma Steady/PrepCom III, see UNCED/PrepCom III

Pronk, Jan (1991), *Advancing towards autonomy*. Speech by the Netherlands Minister for Development Cooperation Jan Pronk, on the occasion of the seminar "Women in development: advancing towards autonomy", the Hague, June 1991. Den Haag: Voorlichtingsdienst Ontwikkelingssamenwerking. In: Informatie, No. 16, 1991 (25 July) (also in reader VENA '92)   42

Pronk, J.P., see also Tweede Kamer der Staten Generaal/J.P.Pronk

R

Radcliffe, Sarah A. with Janet Townsend (1988), *Gender in the Third World. A geographical bibliography of recent work.* (IDS Development Bibliography Series, Sussex, England). (KIT)

Raikes, Philip (1988-1) *Modernizing hunger: famine, food surplus & farm policy in the EEC and Africa.* London: CIIR, James Currey Ltd. ISBN 0-435-08058-X   66

Raikes, Philip (1988-2), *Food shortages and famine. How do they occur, where and to whom.* Chapter 4 in: idem, "Modernizing hunger: famine, food surplus and farm policy in the EEC and Africa."   66, 67

Raintree, John B. (ed.) (1987), *Land, trees and tenure,* proceedings of an international workshop on tenure issues in agroforestry, Nairobi May 27-31 '85. Madison; Nairobi: Land Tenure Center; ICRAF. ISBN 0-934519-01-3   75

Raman, Meenakshi (1991), *Testimony* (on women, health, livelihood and environment in Malaysia) for World Women's Congress for a Healthy Planet, Nov. 8-12, 1991 Miami. Attached: article Martin Khor Kok Peng about UNCED

Ramprasad, Vanaja/People's Health Network (1991), *Population ecology and women's health.* Paper for World Women's Congress for a Healthy Planet, Nov. 8-12, 1991 Miami   62

Rathgeber, Eva M. (1990), WID, WAD, GAD: Trends in research and practice. In: *Journal of Developing Areas.* Vol. 24, 1990 (July). pp 489-502

Redclift, M. (1987/1989), *Sustainable development: exploring the contradictions.* London: Methuen, 1987, (reprinted: London; New York: Routledge) ISBN 0-415-05085-5   46, 54, 96

Redclift, Michael, see also Goodman, David and Michael Redclift

Redeh de Defesa da Especie Humana (1991-1), Mulher, procriacao, ecologia. In: *Gente, Boletim Bimestral da Redeh,* ano 1, No. 1, 1991 (Dez./Jan.) Rio de Janeiro, Brazil (Portuguese)

Redeh de Defesa da Especie Humana, Cadernos da, issue, (1991-2), ano I
numero I 1991, Rio de Janeiro, Brazil (Portuguese)

Reed, David (ed.) (1992), *Structural adjustment and the environment.*
London: Earthscan Publications Ltd. ISBN 1-85383-153-0

Reisen, Mirjam, see Arts, Bas en Mirjam van Reisen

Renner, Magda (1991), *Global homelessness.* Testimony for the World
Women's Congress for a Healthy Planet, Nov. 8-12, 1991 Miami   65

Rijniers, Jeroen (1991), Geboortebeperking als milieumaatregel niet
vanzelfsprekend doelmatig. In: *Internationale Samenwerking.* pp 30-31

Rocheleau, Dianne E. (1991), Gender, ecology and the science of survival:
stories and lessons from Kenya. In: *Agriculture and Human Values.* Vol.
8, No. I, 1991 (January). Fotocopy of manuscript available   73, 92

Rocheleau, Dianne (1990), *Gender complementary and conflict in sustainable
forestry development: a multiple user approach.* Paper presented to IUFRO
World Congress, August 5-11, 1990, Montreal   19, 91

Rocheleau, Dianne (1987), *The user perspective and the agroforestry research
and action agenda.* In: Henri L. Gholz (ed). "Agroforestry: realities,
possibilities and potentials". Dordrecht etc: Martinus Nijhoff
Publishers/ICRAF. pp 59-88   73, 76, 91

Rocheleau, Dianne (1985-1), *Women, environment and development. A
question of priorities for sustainable rural development.* Doc. No. B3/E
Background paper ICRAF, Nairobi. Fotocopy available

Rocheleau, Dianne E. (1985-2), *Women, trees and tenure: implications for
agroforestry research and development.* In: John B. Raintree (ed). "Land,
trees and tenure"   73, 75, 76

Rodda, Annabel (1991), *Women and the environment.* London & New
Jersey: Zed Books/United Nations Non-Governmental Liaison Service.
(Women & World Development Series) ISBN 0-86232-985-X
          19, 30, 55, 59, 69, 73, 91, 97, 98

Roestam, K. Soepardjo (1987), *Some views and comments on "Women and
the World Conservation Strategy".* A contribution to the IUCN workshop
in Gland, Switzerland, 25-27 Nov. 1987   77

Rogers, Barbara (1980), *Women's control of resources.* In: "The domestication
of women, discrimination in developing societies". London: Tavistock
Publications Ltd. pp 122-151

Rojas, M. /FAO (1989), *Women in community forestry: a field guide for project
design and implementation.* Rome: FAO. Fotocopy available

Rojas, Mary/FAO (1988), *Women in community forestry, a field guide for
project design and implementation.* Guidelines. Rome: FAO

Rooney, Nahau (Former Minister Papua New Guinea) (1990), The impact of logging on women. In: *Issues in Women and development*. No. 2, 1990 (March), Asian and Pacific Development Centre. (Extracted from a presentation at the APDC Pacific Workshop, October 1989, pp 6-7). Also in: ISIS International 1991 (information pack)

Royal Netherlands Embassy India (1988-1), *Women in the Netherlands assisted irrigation projects*. New Delhi

Royal Netherlands Embassy India (1988-2), *Women in the Netherlands assisted rural drinking water projects*, New Delhi

Royal Tropical Institute (1993), *Women and development. A bibliography*. Amsterdam: Royal Tropical Institute; Department of Information and Documentation

Royal Tropical Institute (1991), *Reader basic training course on gender: project implementation*. 3-15 Nov. '91 International training course for fieldstaff involved in the implementation of women's projects or the women's components of integrated projects. Amsterdam: Royal Tropical Institute   *38*

Royal Tropical Institute (1988), *Women in rural development, an annotated bibliography*. Amsterdam: Royal Tropical Institute; Department of Information and Documentation. Fotocopy available

Russo, Sandra (et al.) (1989), *Gender issues in agriculture and natural resource management*, by Sandra Russo, Jennifer Bremer-Fox, Susan Poats, Laurene Graig, in cooperation with Anita Spring, edited by Bruce Horwith. Prepared for: Office of Women in Development; Bureau for Program and Policy Coördination; US Agency for International Development. Washington: Robert Nathan Associates Inc   *90, 104*

S

Sa'd, Najwa M. (1988), In a stateless environment (Palestinian Refugees). In: *Women and Environments*. 1988 (Spring) Also in: ISIS International 1991 (information pack)

Safa, Helen I., see Leacock, Eleanor and Helen I. Safa

Safilios-Rotschild, Constantina (1990), Vrouwen en technologie-overdracht. In: *Derde Wereld*. No. 9, 1990. pp 15-18

Safiliou, C. (1991), *Samenvoeging en herziening van de notities "Gender and environment"en "Population growth and environment"van prof.dr ir. Safiliou t.b.v. paragraaf II 2e volgens de bijgewerkte outline Nationale Adviesraad voor Ontwikkelingssamenwerking. C/WG.95/55. Den Haag: NAR, Werkgroep 95, Milieu

Salau, Ademola T. (1991), *Environment and gender: ecological crisis, women and the quest for sustainable development in Africa*. Paper prepared for

CODESRIA Workshop on Gender Analysis and African Social Science, Dakar, September 16-21, 1991

Salleh, Ariel & Maria Mies (1988), Woman, nature & the international division of labour. In: *Thesis-eleven*, 1988. pp 129-139

Sandhu, Ruby and Joanne Sandler (comp.)/International Women's Tribune Centre (1986), *The tech and tools book: a guide to technologies women are using worldwide*. London; New York: Intermediate Technology Publications; IWTC. ISBN 0-946688-17-6

Sandler, Joanne, see Sandhu, Ruby and Joanne Sandler/International Women's Tribune Centre

Sarin, Madhu (1990), Improved stoves, women and domestic energy-the need for a holistic perspective. In: *Forest, Trees and People Newsletter*. No. 9 & 10. pp 16-20. Fotocopy available

Schenk-Sandbergen, Loes (ed.) (1991-1 en 2), reader: *Literatuur bij het kollege "Gender, ekologie en ontwikkeling"*, derde trimester 1991, deel 1 en 11 (New, slightly changed version appeared in 1992)   *35, 62, 70*

Schenk-Sandbergen, L. (1991-3) *Gender and environment: survival strategies of poor households and self-organization of women*. In: Kleinrensink, J.I. "Poverty reduction in India: options & perspectives". The Hague: Ministry of Foreign Affairs, pp 81-88. (DGIS)

Schenk-Sandbergen, Loes (1991-4), *Women and cooking technology: the vicissitudes of improved stove projects in rural Gujarat*. In: Hein Streefkerk and T.K. Moulik (eds) "Managing Rural development". New Delhi: Sage Publications. pp 161-190. In: reader Schenk Sandbergen (1991-1) pp 75-96

Schenk-Sandbergen, Loes (1990), *Empowerment of women: what is its scope in a bilateral development project? The case of the small-scale irrigation project in North-Bengal (Terai area)*. Prepared for 11th European Conference on Modern South Asian Studies. In: reader Schenk-Sandbergen (1991-11) pp 1-29

Schenk-Sandbergen, Loes (1975), *Vervuiling en vuilruimers*. In: "Vuil werk, schone toekomst? Het leven van straatvegers en vuilruimers: een onderzoek in Bulsar (India), verkenningen in Peking, Shanghai, Tientsin en Tangsan (China)". Amsterdam: Van Gennep. pp 63-103 Also in: reader Schenk-Sandbergen (1991-1) pp 183-206

Schlyter, Ann (1990), *Housing and gender: important aspects of urbanization*. In: Satya Datta (ed.), "Third World urbanization: reappraisals and new perspectives". Chapter 11 (KIT)

Schreiber, Goetz, see Molnar, Augusta and Goetz Schreiber

Schrijvers, Joke (1993), *The violence of "development": a choice for intellectuals.* (Inaugural speech delivered by Prof.Dr. Joke Schrijvers, Professor of Development Studies, University of Amsterdam, on friday the 15th of May, 1992). Translated by Lin Pugh, edited by Niala Maharai. Utrecht; New Delhi: International Books and Kali for Women. ISBN 90-6224-9930   *15, 43, 64, 68, 93, 104*

Schrijvers, Joke (1991), *Autonomy as policy: a matter of boundaries?* In: Wim van Zanten (ed), "Across the Boundaries: Women's Perspectives". Papers read in honour of Els Postel-Coster to mark her retirement from the Department of Cultural and Social Studies, University of Leiden, 10-11 January 1991. pp 101-116   *42, 87*

Schrijvers, Joke (1988-1), *Blueprint for undernourishment: the Mahaweli River development scheme in Sri Lanka.* In: B. Agarwal (ed) "Structures of patriarchy: state community & household in modernising Asia". (LEEUW) (Inst. 162)

Schrijvers, Joke (1988-2), *Dialectics of a dialogical ideal; studying down, studying sideways and studying up.* Paper presented at the Bob Scholte Memorial Conference, Amsterdam '88. In: reader '91, Royal Tropical Institute

Schrijvers, Joke (1985), *Mothers for life. Motherhood and marginalization in the North Central Province of Sri Lanka.* Delft: Eburon. ISBN 90-70879-18-2   *40, 42, 87*

Schuler, Margaret (ed.) (1986), *Empowerment and the law. Strategies of Third World women.* Washington DC: OEF International. (Inst. 174) (DGIS)

Schurman, Rachel, see Lappé, Frances Moore and Rachel Schurman

Scott, Adrienne, see Armstrong, Liz and Adrienne Scott/WEED foundation

Scott, James C. (1985), *Weapons of the weak; everyday forms of peasant resistance.* New Haven and London: Yale University Press. ISBN 0-300-03641-8

Secretariat for the Global Consultation on Safe Water and Sanitation for the 1990s (1990), *Creating a safe environment fot better health: water resources, sanitation and the environment.* In: Background Reading No. 1, chapter 2, New Delhi, India, Sept. 10-14, 1990. Fotocopy available

Segal, Lynne (1987), *Compensations of the powerless: the themes of popular feminism.* In: "Is the future female?, troubled thoughts on contemporary feminism". London: Virago, Also in reader Sprenger '91. (Inst. 315) (VENA)

Sen, Gita and Caren Grown/DAWN (1985/87), *Development, crisis, and alternative visions: Third World women's perspectives.* London: Earthscan, 1987. ISBN 1-85383-000-3   *19, 28, 43, 66*

Sen, Gita (1982), *Women workers and the green revolution.* In: Lourdes Beneria (ed.) "Women and development. The sexual division of labour in rural societies". New York: Praeger. pp 29-64. In: reader Schenk-Sandbergen (1991-11), pp 302-320

Sessions, G., see Deval, B. & G. Sessions

Sethi, Harsh (1989), Book review about Vandana Shiva's "Staying alive". (1989). In: *ICSSR Journal of Abstracts and Reviews.* Vol. 18, No. 1, 1989 (Jan./June). pp 157-163. Fotocopy available   *31*

Shallat, Lezak (1990), Take back the earth: women, health and the environment. In: *Women's Health Journal.* No. 20, 1990 (Oct./Nov./Dec.). Latin American and Carribean Women's Health Network, Chile. pp 29-52   *45, 71, 96, 97*

Sharma, K. B. Pandey and K. Natiyal (1985), *The Chipko movement in the Uttarkhand region, Uttar Pradesh, India: women's role and participation.* In: Muntemba, S. "Rural development and women: lessons from the field". Geneva: ILO. Vol. 2, pp 173-193 (LEEUW)

Shiva, Vandana (et al.) (1992), *Biodiversity, social and ecological consequences.* London: ZED Books. ISBN 1-85649-054-8

Shiva, Vandana (1991-1), *The seed and the earth: technology and the colonization of regeneration.* Testimony for World Women's Congress for a Healthy Planet, Nov. 8-12, 1991 Miami   *49*

Shiva, Vandana (1991-2) *Ecology and the politics of survival: conflicts over natural resources in India.* Vandana Shiva in association with J. Bandyopadhay (et al.) New Delhi, Newbury Park, London: Sage Publications; United Nations University Press. ISBN 0-8039-9672-1 *65, 96*

Shiva, Vandana (1990), The rest of reality (Ecofeminism). In: *Ms: American feminist monthly.* 1990 (Nov./Dec.) pp 72-73. Fotocopy available

Shiva, Vandana (1989), *Staying alive: women, ecology and development.* London: Zed Books. ISBN 0-86232-823-3   *17, 30, 43, 49, 63, 69, 96, 97*

Shiva, Vandana (1988-1), *The violence of the green revolution, ecological degradation and political conflict in Punjab.* London: ZED Books. ISBN 0-86232-965-5   *65, 96*

Shiva, Vandana (1988-2), *Reductionist science as an epistemological violence.* In: Ashis Nandy (ed.) "Science, hegemony and violence: a requiem for modernity". New Delhi: Oxford University Press   *49*

Shiva, Vandana, see also Bandyopadhyay, J. and Vandana Shiva, see also Dankelman, Irene and Vandana Shiva, see also Mies, Maria and Vandana Shiva

Shotwell, L.A., see Ofosu-Amaah, Waafas and L.A. Shotwell/WorldWIDE Network

Shrestha, Neeru (1988), *Women as mountain environmental managers in Nepal* (the Case of Kakani Village Panchayat, Centre for Economic Development and Administration, Tribhuvan University Kirtipur, Kathmandu, Nepal, November '88.) Fotocopy available

SIDA, see FAO/SIDA

Sim, Foo Gaik, see Wells, Troth and Foo Gaik Sim

Sims, Jacqueline/WHO (1990), *Women and environment. Effects of environmental factors on women's health.* Prevention of environmental pollution, division of environmental health. Geneva: World Health Organization *19, 71*

Skutsch, M.M. (1987), *Women's access in social forestry, a guide to literature.* (Abbreviated version of a paper entitled "Social forestry for increasing fuel supplies". In: Borg, Brigitte van der, 1989. pp 59-77. Fotocopy available

Skutsch, M.M. (1986), Participation of women in social forestry programmes: problems and solutions. In: *BOS-Newsletter.* Vol. 5, No. 1 No. 13 1986. pp 9-18

Smyke, Patricia (1991), *Women and health.* London: Zed Books (Women and Development Series). ISBN 0-86232-983-3 *70*

Solis, Vivienne and Marta Trejos (1992), *Women and sustainable development in Central America.* San Jose, Costa Rica: IUCN-ORCA

SOMO (Stichting Onderzoek Multinationale Ondernemingen) (1985), *Landbouwmodernisering, het Nederlandse bedrijfsleven en de gevolgen voor vrouwen op het platteland in Zwart Afrika.* Een onderzoek in opdracht van de NCO t.b.v. Platformbijeenkomst over Plattelandsontwikkeling en de positie van de vrouw, 24 April 1985. (VENA)

Sontheimer, Sally (ed.) (1991), *Women and the environment.* A reader: crisis and development in the Third World. London: Earthscan Publications Ltd. ISBN 1-85383-111-5 *35*

Sprenger, Ellen (compiled by) (1991), *Vrouwen, milieu en ontwikkeling.* (reader bij specialisatiekursus Derde Wereld Centrum Nijmegen) *35, 62*

Stamp, Patricia (1989), *Technology, gender and power in Africa.* Ottawa, Ont.: IDRC (Technical study; IDRC-TS63e) ISBN 0-88936-538-5

Starke, Linda/The Centre For Our Common Future (1990), *Signs of hope: working towards our common future.* Oxford & New York: Oxford University Press – ISBN 0-19-285225-6 *25*

Staveren, Irene van (1992), *Over bevolking: een analyse van het denken over bevolkingsgroei en van de praktijk van bevolkingspolitiek.* Utrecht: Stichting OSACI *60*

Stead, Mary (1991), *Women, war and underdevelopment in Nicaragua.* In:

Haleh Afshar "Women, development and survival in the Third World". pp 53-87

Steady, Filomina Chioma, see UNCED/Filomina Chioma Steady/PrepCom II, see UNCED/Filomina Chioma Steady/PrepCom III

Stichting Onderzoek Multinationale Ondernemingen, see SOMO

Stone, Andrew and Augusta Molnar (1986-1), *Issues: women and natural resource management* (draft). Internal document of the World Bank

Stone, A. (ed.) (1986-2), *Bibliography: women and natural resource management in developing countries* (draft, August, 1986) (compiled by Augusta Molnar and Andrew Stone)   72

Strathern, Marilyn, see MacCormack, Carol and Marilyn Strathern

Suliman, Mohamed (ed.) (1991), *Environment, women*. Part 2 of: Alternative Development strategies for Africa: Proceedings of the 1989 Dar es Salaam conference. London: Institute for African Alternatives. (KIT)

Switzer, Margaret A., see Brown, Valerie A. and Margaret A. Switzer

T

Thoenes, Piet (1990), *Milieu en consumptie: blijft meer steeds beter?* In: "Het Milieu: denkbeelden voor de 21ste eeuw". Commissie Lange Termijn Milieubeleid. pp 255-280

Thomas-Emeagwali, Gloria (1991), *Engendering the history of science and technology in Africa*. Paper prepared for CODESRIA Workshop on Gender Analysis and African Social Science, Dakar, September 16-21, 1991

Thorbek, Susanne (1991), Gender in two slum cultures (Thailand, Sri Lanka). In: *Environment and urbanization*. Vol. 3, No. 2, 1991 (Oct.) pp 71-81. Fotocopy available

Thorbek, Suzanne (1990), *A female perspective on urbanization in the Third World*. In: Satya Datta (ed) "Third World urbanization: reappraisals and new perspectives", chapter 12

Tinker, Irene (1990), *Persistent inequalities: women and world development*. New York & Oxford: Oxford University Press. ISBN 0-19506-158-6 (VENA)   38

Tolba, M.K. (1985), *An alliance with nature: women and the earth's traditions*. Statement to World Conference to Review and Appraise the Achievements of the UN Decade for Women, Nairobi 15-24 July '85 (also in Global Assembly, conferencemap, 1991)

Townsend, J.G., see Momsen, J.H. and J.G. Townsend, see Radcliffe, Sarah A. with Janet Townsend

Trejos, Marta/CEFEMINA (1991), *Building the future starting from the needs of the present*. Paper for the 20th World Conference of the Society for International Development, Regional seminar III: Population, Women and Natural Resource Management May 6-9, 1991 Amsterdam

Trejos, Marta, see also Solis, Vivienne and Marta Trejos

Tribune, the, issue: (1991), "Women, environment and development". Newsletter, No. 47, 1991 (Sept.)

Tribune, the, issue: (1990), a women and development quarterly, issue: "Women and new technologies". An organizing manual, No. 44, 1990 (march) YWCA/IWTC Switzerland/USA

Tuana, Nancy (ed.) (1989), *Feminism and science.* Bloomington and Indianapolis: Indiana University Press. (Inst. 174/126) (VENA)   *49*

Tulchin, Joseph S. (ed.) *Habitat, health and development. A new way of looking at cities in the Third World.* Colorado: Lynne Rienner Publications. pp 105-120. Fotocopy available

Tweede Kamer der Staten Generaal (1991), *Milieu en internationale handel.* Brief van Staatssecretaris Y. van Rooy van Economische Zaken 30 Aug. '91. Tweede Kamer, Vergaderjaar 1990-1991, 21951, No. 2. Den Haag: SDU Uitgeverij

Tweede Kamer der Staten-Generaal/J.P. Pronk (1990), *Een wereld van verschil. Nieuwe kaders voor ontwikkelingssamenwerking in de jaren negentig.* Tweede Kamer, vergaderjaar 1990-1991, 21813, No. 1-2. Den Haag: SDU Uitgeverij   *42, 83*

U

UN (1972), *Declaration of the United Nations Conference on the Human Environment, Stockholm, 5-15 June 1972.* pp 3-5. In: Reader Development Studies "People, environment and development: the urgent need for transformation, 1992/1993"/InDRA-UVA

UN (1991), *The world's women, 1970-1990: trends, and statistics.* New York: UN (VENA)

UN (1986), *The Nairobi Forward Looking Strategies for the Advancement of Women,* as adopted by the World Conference to Review and Appraise the Achievements of the United Nations Decade for Women: Equality, Development and Peace, Nairobi, Kenya 15-26 July '85. UN Department of Public Information, Division for Economic and Social information
      24, 27, 32, 57, 78, 79

UN/INSTRAW, see. INSTRAW

UNASYLVA, an international journal of forestry and forest industries, issue (1984), Vol. 36, No. 146, 1984/4. Theme/special issue on "Women in Forestry"/FAO ISSN 0251-1053

UNCED (1992-1), *The Declaration of Rio de Janeiro on Environment and Development* Conches: UNCED Secretariat (in: InDRA Reader 1993)
20, 26, 28, 61

UNCED (1992-2), *Agenda 21* Conches: UNCED Secretariat. Available on floppy disk
20, 26, 28, 104

UNCED/PrepCom IV (1992), *Women, environment and development in UNCED:* discussion paper for the preparations of UNCED in Rio de Janeiro, June 1992 (in particular PrepCom IV in New York, March 1992)

UNCED/PrepCom III (1991-1) *Women in environment and development.* Preparations for the United Nations Conference on Environment and Development on the basis of general assembly resolution 44/228 and taking into account other relevant general assembly resolutions. Cross-sectoral issues. (e.g. by the Netherlands on behalf of the States Members of the United Nations that are members of the European Community) 19 August '91
28, 34, 79

UNCED/PrepCom III (1991-2), *Daily Press Bulletin No. 13/2* Resolution focusses on women's issues, Inter Press Service coverage of Prepcom III

UNCED/Filomina Chioma Steady/PrepCom II (1991-1), *Emerging gender issues at UNCED* Second Preparatory Committee, Geneva 18 March-5 April 1991, UNCED, Switzerland

UNCED/Filomina Chioma Steady/PrepCom III (1991-2), *From emergence to visibility. A decision on women in PrepCom III*
34, 79

UNCED, see also Alders, J.G.M./UNCED

UNCHS (Habitat) (1989-1), *Women and human settlements development.* Nairobi: United Nations Centre for Human Settlements. ISBN 92-1-131118-7

UNCHS (Habitat) (1989-2), *Urbanization and sustained development in the Third World: an unrecognized global issue,* Nairobi: United Nations Centre for Human Settlements (Inst. 162)

UNDP/UNICEF (1984), *Insights from field practice: how women have been and could be involved in water supply and sanitation at the community level.* Prepared by Ma Yansheng and Mary Elmendorf. New York: United Nations Development Programme/UNICEF

UNDP (1985-1), *Is there a better way? Promotion and support for women's participation in the International Drinking Water Supply and Sanitation Decade '81-'90.* New York: United Nations Development Programme

UNDP (1985-2), *Resolution: women and the environment.* (World Conference to Review and Appraise the Achievements of the UN Decade for Women "Equality, Development, and Peace". (see statement Tolba in "Global Assembly" conferencemap, 1991)

Viegas, Philip and Geeta Menon (1989), *The impact of environmental degradation on people*. New Delhi: Indian Social Institute

Voices from Africa, issue (1989), on women, No. 1, 1989. Geneva: UNCTAD/NGLS

VROM/Ministry of Housing, Physical Planning and Environment (1991), *Netherlands national report to UNCED 1992: United Nations Conference on Environment and Development*. Den Haag: VROM   *83*

VROM/Ministry of Housing, Physical planning and Environment (1990), *National Evironmental Policy Plan Plus*. (NEPP-plus 1990-1994) Den Haag: VROM. (VROM 00278/10-90 7583/129)   *83*

VVAO/Vakgroep Vrouwenstudies in de Landbouw/LUW (1987), *Vrouwen-recht-op-onderdak, verslag van de studiedag over de habitat problematiek van vrouwen in krottenwijken in de Derde Wereld*, 31 Januari 1987

VVAO Mededelingen, issue (1990), "Vrouwen en energie". 56 (1990) 6

W

Wadehra, Renu and Manab Chakraborty (1987), *Deforestation and afforestation: women's response in Uttarakhand, India*. Amsterdam: Netherlands IUCN Committee

Wallace, Tina and Candida March (ed.) (1991), *Changing perceptions. Writings on gender and development*. Oxford: Oxfam Publishers (VENA) *38*

Walsum, Edith van (1991), *Gender methodology in agricultural projects: reader*. Wageningen: Agricultural University, Department of Gender Studies in Agriculture

Walsum, Edith van (ed.) (1989), *Gender issues in agriculture: a reader*. Wageningen: Agricultural University, Department of Gender Studies in Agriculture   *75*

Walter, Renate (1991), *Threats to a healthy planet and its inhabitants: industrial and military pollution*. Testimony for World Women's Congress for a Healthy Planet, Nov. 8-12, 1991 Miami   *65*

Wanawake, issue, (1991), tijdschrift over vrouwen in het ontwikkelingswerk. Themanummer Milieu. Jrg. 6, No. 1, 1991 (April). Wageningen: Vrouwengroep CON   *35*

War on Want, see WEN/War on Want

Wariken, P. F. (et al.) (1989), *The impact of economic and agricultural policies on women in agriculture: four casestudies*. Washington, U.S.: Agency for International Development. (Agricultural Policy Analysis Project Technical Document; No. 506)

Waring, Marilyn (1988-1), *If women counted, a new feminist economics.*
London: Macmillan Publishers ISBN 0-333-49262-5   *58, 64, 68*
Waring, Marilyn (1988-2), *Your economic theory makes no sense: economics and the exploitation of the planet.* In: Marilyn Waring, "If women counted". Chapter 10, pp 250-275   *58, 64*
Warren, K. J. (1990), The power and the promise of ecological feminism. In: *Environmental Ethics.* Vol. 12, No. 2, 1990 pp 125-146
Warren, Karen J. (1987), Feminism and ecology: making connections. In: *Environmental Ethics.* Vol. 9, No. 1, 1987 (spring). pp 3-20. Fotocopy available   *47, 49, 51, 52*
Warwick, Fox (1989), The deep ecology-ecofeminism debate and its parallels. In: *Environmental Ethics,* 11 (1989) pp 5-25
Watkins, K. (1991), Agricultural & food security in the GATT Uruguay Round. In: *Review of African Political Economy.* No. 50, 1991. pp 38-50 (Inst. 162)
WCED, Reconvened (1992), *Our common future. Reconvened World Commission on Environment and Development,* 22-24 April 1992, London. Geneva: Centre for Our Common Future
WCED/World Commission on Environment and Development (1987), *Our common future.* Oxford: Oxford University Press   *25, 32, 44, 48, 60, 78, 83*
WEDNET (et al.) (1989), *Women, Environment and Development Network: report of first meeting.* (Greenhills hotel, Nyeri, Kenya 26-29 June 1989) *74*
WEDNEWS, issue (1990/1991), a newsletter of the Women, Environment and Development NETWORK, an ELCI project. Issue No. 1, 1990, No. 2/3, 1990-91   *74*
WEDO (1992-1), *Community Report Card. An information and organizing tool for evaluating the real environmental health and social justice status of your community.* New York: Women's Environment & Development Organization   *91*
WEDO (1992-2) *WEDO Comments on PrepCom IV. Documents based on "Women's Action Agenda 21".* World Women's Congress for a Just and Healthy Planet. New York: Women's Environment and Development Organization (Both Ends)   *104*
WEDO (forthcoming), Analysis of women in "Agenda 21" and other UNCED documents. Title yet unknown. New York: Women's Environment & Development Organization   *81*
WEDO, see also World Women's Congress for a Healthy Planet/WEDO, see also Women's Environment & Development Organization/WEDO
WEED Foundation, see Armstrong, Liz and Adrienne Scott/WEED Foundation

Kate Young

countries signed an agreement allowing for
of 20,000 Cubans annually to the United S
the gradual return of the undesirables to
meantime Cuba–U.S. relations had worsen
United States invaded the island of Grena
killing a number of Cubans and expelling t
of the Cuban aid force from the island.

Although some overall improvement in Cu
tions could be noted since the revolution, t
embargo imposed in the early 1960s remain
in force, and there were few signs of thaw
1980s. U.S. probes concerning the conditio
prisoners in Cuba and the propaganda broa
from the U.S. Radio Martí since 1985 conti
agitation. Cuba began a phased withdrawal
from Angola in 1989.

Cuba continued to lean heavily upon the
for support of its economy, although that
tightened its trade policy with Cuba, compou
stringent economic conditions on the island.
relations deteriorated somewhat as a result
alization in the late 1980s of Soviet politic
and social policies, which the Cuban hierarch
prove, despite movement in that direction b
Eastern-bloc nations.

For later developments in the history of C
Britannica Book of the Year section in t
WORLD DATA ANNUAL.

Weimin, Chen/China Environment News (1991), *Chinese women journalists shoulder an impetative task.* Handout World Women's Congress for a Healthy Planet, Nov. 8-12, 1991 Miami

Wells, Troth and Foo Gaik Sim (1987), *Till they have faces: women as consumers.* Penang, Malaysia: Consumers Association (Both Ends)

WEN/War on Want (1989-1), *Women, environment, development. Seminar report* (7 March 1989) London: The Women's Environmental Network; War on Want

WEN (1989-2), *Managua Declaration.* Women's Environmental Network. In: ISIS International 1991 (information pack)

Whitehead, Ann (1991), *Notes for workshop on gender relations and agrarian change.* CODESRIA Workshop on Gender Analysis and African Social Science, Dakar, September 16-21, 1991

Whitehead, Ann (1990), *Food crisis and gender conflict in the African countryside.* In: Bernstein, Henry (et al.) (ed) "The food question: profits versus people?", 1990 pp 54-68

Whitehead, Ann (1985), *The green revolution and women's work in the Third World.* In: Wendy Faulkner and Eric Arnold (ed), "Smothered by Invention; Technology in Women's lives". pp 183-199

WHO, see Sims, Jacqueline/WHO

Wickramasinghe, Anoja (1991-1), *The user's perspective in selecting tree species for farming systems.* In: "Multipurpose tree species in Sri Lanka; research and development: Proceedings of the second regional workshop, organized by National Research Committee on Multipurpose Tree Species and Winrock International", F/FRED, Bangkok, Thailand, 5-7 April 1991/Ed. H.P.M. Gunasena. pp 164-176

Wickramasinghe, Anoja (1991-2), *Gender issues in the management of homegardens: a case study of Kandyan homegardens in Sri Lanka.* Paper presented at the "International symposium on Man-made Community, Integrated Land-use and Biodiversity in the Tropics", Kunming Institute of Ecology, Academia Sinica, 26-31st October 1991, Jinghong Hotel, Xishuanbanna, Yunnan, People's Republic of China

Wickramasinghe, Anoja (1989), *The woman's role in the rural household and agriculture in Sri Lanka.* Paper for a workshop on "Gender and development", April 16-21 '89, Commonwealth Geographical Bureau, University of Newcastle Upon Tyne, England   72

WID Expert group task force, see DAC/WID Expert group task force

Wieberdink, Ange/InDRA (1991), *Linking women, environment and development (WED). Will it produce a surplus value?* Introduction to the basic training course on Gender, Royal Tropical Institute Nov. '91, Amsterdam   *19, 105*

Wiertsema, Wiert (1991), *Ecology and social justice: strategies for change.* Paper for El Taller/Third World Network Environment Workshop, 25-31 July 1991. In: Reader InDRA (1991)   *16*

Wignaraja, Ponna/UNICEF (1990), *Women, poverty and resources.* New Delhi etc.: SAGE Publications/UNICEF. ISBN (US) 0-8039-9624-1 / (India) 81-7036-167-2

Wijk-Sijbesma, Christine van (1985), *Participation of women in water supply and sanitation, roles and realities.* The Hague: IRC (International Reference Centre for Community Water Supply and Sanitation) (Technical Paper; No. 22) ISBN 90-6687-006-0   *70*

Williams, Paula (1991), *Women, children and forest resources in Africa: casestudies and issues.* Paper prepared for "Women and children first" symposium ..., Geneva May 27-30, 1991. UNCED

Wolfson, D.J. and D. Ghai (1987), *The rural energy crisis, women's work and basic needs.* Proceedings of a Workshop sponsored by the ILO and the Institute of Social Studies, The Hague, April 1987. Geneva, Switzerland: International Labour Office

Women and Environments, issue (1991), Women and environmental activity: special issue (on UNCED). Vol. 13, No. 2, 1991. pp 3-76   *35*

Women and habitat workshop. (1985), Forum '85. NGO meeting held in conjunction with UN Conference to Review and Appraise the Achievements of the Decade for Women. Nairobi, Kenya 10-19 July 1985 organised by UNCHS. Compiled by Diana Lee-Smith

Women, Environment, Development, see WEN

Women, fishery and the marine environment, (1991), literaturelist compiled by Olga Nieuwenhuis September 1991

Women in Action, issue (1991), Women speak out on the environment. Vol. 4/1991

Women of Power, issue (1991), A magazine of feminism, spirituality & politics, e.g. issue spring '91 The living earth

"Women's Action Agenda 21", see World Women's Congress ... 1991 and 1992

Women's Health Journal, issue (1990), Take back the earth. Women, health and the environment. No. 20. Latin American and Caribbean Women's Health Network (esp. pp 30-52)

Women's World/ISIS-WICCE, issue (1988), *Debt crisis.* No. 17, March 1988

Women's World/ISIS-WICCE, issue (1986), *Appropriate technology for our earth.* No. 12, December 1986

Wood Energy News, special issue on women. (1990), Vol. 5, No. 1, April 1990. Issued by the Project Regional Wood Energy Development Programme in Asia (GCR/RAS/131/NET). Fotocopy available

World Bank, see Clones, Julia/World Bank, see ESMAP/World Bank

World Commission on Environment and Development, see WCED

World Women's Congress for a Healthy Planet /WEDO (1992), *Official report, including "Women's Action Agenda 21" and "Findings of the tribunal".* New York: Women's Environment and Development Organization   27, 28, 33, 51, 55, 64, 67, 71, 98, 104

World Women's Congress for a Healthy Planet (1991-1), *8-12 November 1991, Miami, Florida, USA / Women's International Policy Action Committee on Environment and Development (IPAC).* Announcements, programmes, lists of participants, congress results, speeches, testimonies, press releases and tribunals (on tape) available at InDRA (see also: Arias, Briones, Walter, Renner, Engo-Tjeda, Antrobus, Shiva, Bertell)
                                                                27, 28, 33, 55

World Women's Congress for a Healthy Planet (1991-2), *Women and children of the rainforest: presentation and discussion of the impact of deforestation on women and children in communities that depend on the rainforest and an appeal for support from Sarawak women.* Workshop with presentations by Meenakshi Raman, Sahabat Alam/Friends of the Earth Malaysia; Kazuko Matsue, Japan Tropical Forest Action Network; Pamela Wellner, Rainforest Action Network, USA

WorldWIDE Network (1991/1993), *WorldWIDE directory of women in environment.* Washington: WorldWIDE Network

WorldWIDE Network, see also Ofosu-Amaah, Waafas and L.A. Shotwell/WorldWIDE Network

YWCA Energy and Environment Newsletter, issue (1988), "Environment and health: appropriate technology and health. May 1988 World Environment Day, June 5 1988" (Young Women's Christian Association)

Zimmerman, Michael E. (1987), Feminism, deep ecology and environmental ethics. In: *Environmental Ethics.* Vol. 9, No. 1, 1987 (Spring). pp 20-44. Fotocopy available   47, 52

Information about libraries and magazines

Libraries

ARBOR: Arboretum library Wageningen, Generaal Foulkesweg 64, 6703 BV Wageningen, tel. 08370-82542.

Both Ends: Damrak 28-30, 1012 LJ Amsterdam, tel. 020-6230823/6261732.

DGIS: Ministry of Foreign Affairs, Bezuidenhoutseweg 67, 2500 EB Den Haag, tel. 070-3484345.

IIAV: Internationaal Informatiecentrum en Archief voor de Vrouwenbeweging, Keizersgracht 10, Amsterdam, tel. Library: 020-6244268.

ISS: Institute of Social Studies, Badhuisweg 251, 2509 LS Den Haag, tel. 070-3510100/0124.

KIT: Royal Tropical Institute: Mauritskade 63, 1092 AD Amsterdam, tel. 020-5688711/8474.

LEEUW: Leeuwenborch Library, Hollandseweg 1, 6706 KN Wageningen, tel. 08370-82493.

LUW: Agricultural University Wageningen Jan Kopshuis, Generaal Foulkesweg 19, 6703 BK Wageningen, tel. 08370-82163.

Milieudefensie: Damrak 26, 1012 LJ Amsterdam, tel. 020-6221366 (Opened on fridays 9.00-16.00 h.).

UB: Universiteits Bibliotheek UVA, Singel 425, Amsterdam, tel. 020-5252311.

VENA: Wassenaarseweg 52, Kamer 4B21, 2300 RB Leiden, tel. 071-273492.

Institutes at the University of Amsterdam

Inst. 126: Instituut voor filosofie, Vendelstraat 8, Amsterdam, tel.
020-5254555

Inst. 132: Instituut voor Fonetische Wetenschappen, Herengracht 338,
Amsterdam, tel. 020-5252186

Inst. 138: Historisch Sem. Spuistraat 134, Amsterdam, tel. 020-5254427

Inst. 141: Documentatiecentrum voor Nieuwste Geschiedenis, o.z.
Achterburgwal 237, Amsterdam, tel. 020-5253009

Inst. 142: Economisch Sem. van de Faculteit der Sociale Wetenschappen,
Oudezijds Achterburgwal 237, Amsterdam, tel. 020-5252403/2404

Inst. 143: Centrale Bibliotheek Psychologisch Lab., Roeterstraat 15,
Amsterdam, tel. 020-5256732

Inst. 157: Sociologisch Instituut, Oude Hoogstraat 24, Amsterdam, tel.
020-5253982

Inst. 160: Bibliotheek Agrarische en Ontwikkelingseconomie, for address
etc, see Inst. 323

Inst. 162: Sociaal Geografisch Instituut, Roeterstraat 11, Amsterdam, tel.
020-5254273

Inst. 163: IVAM (Interfacultaire Vakgroep Milieukunde), Nieuwe
Prinsengracht 130, Amsterdam, tel. 020-5255072/5256206

Inst. 164: Planologisch Demografisch Instituut, for address etc, see No. 323,
Piersonbibliotheek.

Inst. 166: Andragologie, Grote Bickerstraat 72, 2ᵉ etage, tel.
020-5251227/5550360

Inst. 168: Pedagogisch Didaktisch Instituut, for address, etc. see Inst. 166

Inst. 173: Amerika Instituut, Plantage Muidergracht 12, Amsterdam, tel.
020-5254380

Inst. 174: CEDLA, Keizersgracht 395-397, Amsterdam, tel. 020-5253248

Inst. 175: Antropologisch Sociologisch Centrum, Afd. Zuid- en Zuidoost
Azië, o.z. Achterburgwal 185, Amsterdam, tel. 020-5252447

Inst. 176: Antropologisch Sociologisch Centrum, Afd. Culturele
Antropologie, for address etc. see No. 175

Inst. 177: Instituut voor Wetenschap der Politiek, o.z. Achterburgwal 237,
Amsterdam, tel. 020-5252403

Inst. 184: Juridisch Instituut, Oude Manhuispoort 4, tel. 020-5253843

Inst. 189: Sem. v. Volkenrecht en Internationale Betrekkingen,
Turfdraagsterpad 1, BG Geb. 1, 2ᵉ etage, tel. 020-5252161

Inst. 242: Artis-Bibliotheek (Plantagebibliotheek), Plantage Middenlaan 45,
Amsterdam, tel. 020-5256614

Inst. 244: Afdeling Diergedrag, Plantage Middenlaan 45, Amsterdam, tel. 020-5256614

Inst. 264: Bibliotheek der Scheikunde, Nieuwe Achterburgwal 166, tel. 020-5256501

Inst. 286: Wetenschap en Samenleving, Subfaculteit Natuurkunde, Nieuwe Achtergracht 170, tel. 020-5255887

Inst. 310: Faculteit Economie en Econometrie, for address, etc. see No. 323 Piersonbibliotheek

Inst. 315: Algemene Pedagogiek, IJsbaanpad 9, Amsterdam, tel. 020-6644331

Inst. 323: Prof. Mr. N.G. Piersonbibliotheek (FEE/FRW), Roeterstraat 11, Amsterdam, tel. 020-5254273.

Location of Magazines

The *Italics* = specialized in GED, Women & Development, or Environment & Development.

Agricultural administration & extension: LEEUW
Alternative Treaties Bulletin, bimonthly: InDRA from 1992.
Alternatives, social transformation and human governance: Inst. 177
AT Source: Both Ends
A Propos: Inst. 315
Balancing the future: Both Ends
Behavioral and social sciences librarian: Inst. 143
BOS-Newsletter: ARBOR
BOVO-Nieuwsbrief: InDRA
DAWN Informs: Both Ends
Daedalus, journal of the American Academy of Arts and Science: Inst. 173
Derde Wereld: InDRA/Inst. 162
Development, journal of the Society of International Development: InDRA
Development and Change: ISS / InDRA from 1991
Down to earth, Science and environment fortnightly: InDRA from 1992.
Earthwatch: Both Ends
Ecoforum: Both Ends
Ecologist, the, the journal of the post industrial age: Inst. 163/126/323 /
    Milieudefensie / InDRA from 1992
Economic and political weekly: Inst. 323/175
Ekistics: Inst. 164
Environmental Ethics, an interdisciplinary journal dedicated to the
    philosophical aspects of environmental problems: ISS / LEEUW / Inst.
    126/163
Environment and Urbanization: Library of PDI/SGI
Femconsult Newsletter: IIAV
Forest, Trees and People Newsletter: Both Ends
Gender Studies in Agriculture, a journal of Abstracts: LEEUW / InDRA from
    1990
Hypatia, a Journal of Feminist Philosophy: IIAV / Inst. 126
IDS Bulletin: Inst. 175/174/310
Impact, magazine on environment and development: KIT
IMWOO Bulletin: InDRA
INSTRAW News: InDRA from Summer 1989
International Labour Review: Inst. 143 / UB

Issues in Women and Development: IIAV
Journal of Developing Areas: Inst. 162
Journal of Peasant Studies: Inst. 162/175/323
Journal of Rural Studies: Inst. 162
Lover, literatuuroverzicht voor de vrouwenbeweging: InDRA from 1991
Manushi, a journal about women in society: UB
Ms: American feminist monthly: Inst. 166 (jrg.1976-1987)
Nation, the: (Inst. 173)
Praxis, a quarterly journal: Inst. 126 (jrg. 1970/1974)
Review of African Political Economy: Inst. 162/176
Science and Public Policy: Inst. 264/286
Thesis eleven: UB
Tijdschrift voor vrouwenstudies: Inst. 157 / IIAV
Tribune, the: Both Ends / InDRA from No. 41 (March 1989)
UNASYLVA, an international journal of forestry and forest industries:
    University Library Leiden
VENA Newsletter: InDRA
Voices from Africa: InDRA 1989/1990
Wanawake: InDRA
WED-NEWS,magazine from Women, Environment and Development Network
    (WEDNET), InDRA Issue No. 1 (1990), No. 2/3 (1990/1991)
Wetenschap en Samenleving: UB / Inst. 166/264/286
WIDE Bulletin: InDRA from 1991
Women and environments: Inst. 162 / InDRA from 1991
Women of power: IIAV
Women's Environmental Network Newsletter,the: Both Ends
Women's World (Isis/WICCE): ISS
Women in Action: InDRA
Wood Energy News: ARBOR
World Development: Inst. 310 / DGIS
Worldwatch Paper: Milieudefensie
WorldWIDE News: World Women in Environment: InDRA from December
    1988 – January 1991.
YWCA Energy and Environment Newsletter: (–).

Alphabetical index for the bibliography

This index is meant to have an overview of the publications focused on specific issues such as agriculture, forestry, migration, etc. It refers to the bibliography only, and can be used in addition to the text in this guide. In the bibliography itself one finds the numbers of the pages where the publications are discussed or mentioned.

Smyke 1991
WHO 1984
Wickramasinghe 1989
Women's Health Journal 1990
YWCA 1988

Labour, employment
Afshar 1991
Cecelski 1987-1-2
ILO 1985
Leacock & Safa 1986
Mies 1986
Momsen & Townsend 1987
Muller & Plantenga 1987/1990
Muntemba 1985
Pearson 1988
Rathgeber 1990
Salleh and Mies 1988
Sen 1982
VVAO 83-1-2
Wignaraja 1990
See also *agriculture, a.o.*

Macroeconomics and related issues
Alkemade et al 1989
Amstel 1987
Beneria & Sen 1984
Bernstein et al 1990
Brown 1991
Bruyn, de 1992
Heyzer 1991
INSTRAW 1985-1
Jain 1991
JUNIC-NGO 1988-1-2
Mies 1986
Lappé & Collins 1986
Mies 1986
Sen & Grown-DAWN 1985
SOMO 1985
Tweede Kamer 1991
Vickers 1991
Wariken 1989
Waring 1988-1-2
Watkins 1991

World Women's Congress 1992
See also *macroeeconomic systems of accounting, and debts.*

Macroeconomic systems of accounting, national income accounting
Appleton 1991
Bij, van der 1991
Boserup 1970
Buechner et al 1990
Bushwick 1985
Charkiewicz 1993
Drake 1990
Group of Green Economists 1992
Harcourt 1991-1
Hueting et al 1991
Kennedy in Linggard & Moberg 1990
Waring 1988-1-2.

Management of natural resources: see *natural resources.*

Methodology: *see planning or research.*

Migration, refugees
Bennet 1991
Forbes Martin 1991
Palmer 1985
Renner 1991
Sa'd 1988
See also *militarism and war.*

Militarism and war
Antrobus 1991-2
Bennet 1991
Bertell 1991
Forbes Martin 1991
Harcourt 1991
JUNIC-NGO 1988-3
Reardon 1985
Stead 1991

Walter 1991
Waring 1988.

Movements, networks, organizations; countervailing power
Agarwal, A. 1987 (India)
Agarwal B. 1988-1/1989 (India)
Antrobus 91-1 (DAWN)
Bakhteari 1988
Bandhyopadyay & Shiva 1987
  (Chipko)
Berg 1990
Bhatt 1989
Both Ends 1992
Campen, van 1988 (the Netherlands)
Chambers 1985 (India)
Dankelman and Davidson 1988
  (casestudies)
Davis, K. et al 1991
Dietrich 88-1-3 (India)
Ecoforum 1990
Global Assembly (casestudies)
Guha 1991 (India)
Haüsler and Charkiewicz-Pluta
  1991-1
Hedley 1990
ISIS International 1990 & 1991
Kishwar & Vanita 1984
Maathai 1984/1988 (Green Belt)
Molyneux 1987 (Nicaragua)
Moser (Ecuador)
Muller & Plantenga 1987/1990
  (urban)
Omvedt 1992 (India)
Rodda 1991 (casestudies)
Schenk-Sandbergen 1990/1991-3
  (India)
Schuler 1986
Scott 1985
Sharma & Natiyal 1985 (Chipko)
Sontheimer 1991
Tribune 1991
UNIFEM 1991 (casestudies)
Vermeulen 1992 (the Netherlands)

WEDNET 1989-1-2
Women & Environments 1991
World WIDE Network 1991.

Natural resources, and women, gender, compilations of casestudies
general
Aidoo 1988
Dankelman 1991-1
Dankelman and Davidson 1988
Davidson 1989
Dehlot 1991
ELC/Forum 1985 1986
Global Assembly 1992 and 1991
Hedley 1990
IUCN 1987-1-2
Jommo 1992
Loudiyi 1991 (bibl.)
Rodda 1991
Rogers 1980
Royal Trop.(1988, bibl.)
Sontheimer 1991
Sprenger 1991
Stock 1982
Stone 1986-2 (bibl.)
Stone & Molnar 1986-1
Verkruijsse et al 1992 (bibl.)
WEN 1990

India
Agarwal, A. 1992
Agarwal, A. & Narain 1985
Agarwal, B. 1986/1988 1-2/1989
Anand 1983
CSE 1985/1991
Fernandes 1987
Kelkar 1991
Nathan 1990
Schenk-Sandbergen 1991-1-2 (reader)
Sethi 1989
Shiva 1988/1989/1991-255
Wignaraja 1990

171

others
Baxter 1991 (Sudan)
Hassan (Egypt)
ICIMOD 1989 (Nepal)
Jong 1990 (Sudan)
Khasiani 1992 (Africa)
Kreiman 1985 (Argentina)
Leach 1991 (Sierra Leone)
Murphy 1985 (Brazil)
Pandey 1985 (Nepal)
Shrestu (Nepal)
Solis & Trejos 1992 (Central
    America)
Stamp 1987 (Africa)
Wickramasinghe 1989/1991-2 (Sri
    Lanka)
Williams 1991 (Africa)
See also *agriculture / forestry.*

Philosophy: *see ecofeminism a.o. /*
environmental philosophy / science,
feminist critique of.

Planning methodology, GED
manuals a.o.
Boesveld 1990 and in Rodda 1991
Canadian Council 1990
    (environment)
CCIC et al 1991 (gender)
Commonwealth Secreatriat 1992
    (GED manual)
Davidson 1990
Feldstein & Poats 1989
Gura 1985 (extension)
ICIMOD 1989
Leach 1991
Leeuwen 1990
Martin Brown & El-Hinnawi 1988
Ministry of Foreign Affairs
    1989/1990
Molnar & Schreiber 1989
Molyneux 1987
Moser 1989-1 (gender planning)
Moser and Levy 1986

Overholt 1985
Poats et al 1988 and 1989
Postel and Boesveld 1989
Postel 1990
Rojas 1989
Russo 1989 (GED manual)
Walsum, van 1991
See also *research.*

Policy: see *development policy.*

Pollution, poisoning
Armstrong & Scott 1992
Barten 1992
Bertell 1991 and in Linggard &
    Moberg 1990
Campen, van 1988
Carson 1962
Costello et al 1989
Ling 1989
Hynes 1989-1
Walter 1991.

Population, consumption
Blaikie & Brookfield 1987
Chitepo 1991
Corral 1991
Dasgupta 1985
DAWN-concerned scholars 1992
Joekes 1989
Lappé & Schurman 1988
Mamdani 1981
Mies 1991
Mwalo 1991
Nederlandse Vrouwen Raad 1990
Oever, van den 1991
Pollard et al 1992
Postel 1989
Ramprasad 1991
Redeh 1991-1-2
Rijniers 1991
Staveren, van 1991
Thoenes 1990
Trejos 1991

Agarwal, A.-CSE 1991
Agarwal, A. & Narain 1989
Agarwal, B. 1986/1989
Arts & v. Reisen 1988
Bhasin et al 1991
Blaikie & Brookfield 1987
Braidotti et al 1993
Chambers 1988/1987,
Chambers et al 1989-2
Chowdry 1989
Conroy and Litvinov 1988
Commissie Ecologie 1986
Court, de la 1990
CSE 1991
Dankelman 1991-1
Daly & Cobb 1990
FOOD 2000 1987
Foster 1986
Frijns & Hazeu 1991 (reader)
Hecht & Cockburn 1989
Goodman & Redclift 1991
INDRA 1993 (reader)
Leach, M. and Mearns 1991-2
Malnes 1990
Milbrath 1989
Ministry of Foreign Affairs 1991-2
Mitlin 1992 (guide to literature)
NAR 1992 and 1991
Redclift 1987
Starke 1990
UNEP 1992 and 1988
VROM 1992
Worldwatch Institute 1992
World Women's Congress 1991 and
    1992
Wiertsema 1991
See also *environmental philosophy.*

Technology
Bicocci and Ochs (1990, bibl.)
Eldredge et al 1990 (bibl.)
Faulkner 1985
Hassan 1988
Hynes 1989-1-2

INSTRAW 85-1
Safilios Rothshild 1990
Sandhu 1986
Schenk Sandbergen 1991-4
Shiva 1991-1
Shiva et al 1992
Thomas-Emeagwali 1991
Tribune, the 1990
Veken & Hernandez 1986.

**Urban environment and gender,
habitat**
Bonsink 1989
Brydon & Chant 1989
DAC-Expert Group 1990
Datta 1990
Dietrich 1990
Ekistics 1985
Environment and Urbanization 1991
Forum 1985, 1985-1
Gooier 1986
Hardoy et al 1990
IYSH 1987
Kalpaga 1985
Kjellberg Bell 1991 (guide to
    literature)
Letsch 1990/1993
Moser 1987-1/1989-2
Moser and Castleton 1991
Moser and Peake 1987
Muller & Plantenga 1987/1990
Schenk-Sandbergen 1975
Schlyter 1990
Thorbek 1990 and 91
Tulchin
UNCHS 1989-1-2
VENA Newsletter 1990
VVAO 1987
See also *health a.o.*

War: see *Militarism and war.*

Watersupply and Sanitation
Briscoe 1986